Freya

P · O · C · K · E · T · S

ANCIENT EGYPT

MUMMIFIED HEAD

ANUBIS, THE JACKAL GOD OF EMBALMING

OUTER AND INNER MUMMY CASES

FOOT CASE FROM A MUMMY

P · O · C · K · E · T · S

ANCIENT EGYPT

Written by
SCOTT STEEDMAN

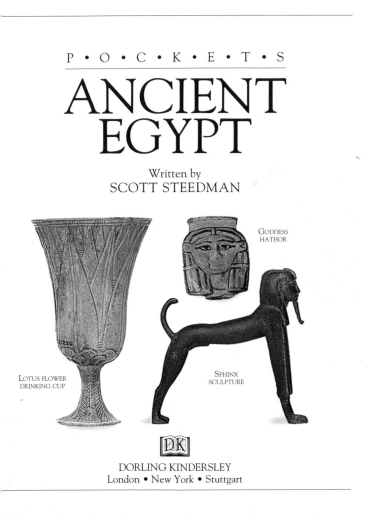

GODDESS
HATHOR

LOTUS FLOWER
DRINKING CUP

SPHINX
SCULPTURE

DK

DORLING KINDERSLEY
London • New York • Stuttgart

A DORLING KINDERSLEY BOOK

Project editor Linda White
Art editor Ann Cannings
Assistant designer Kate Eagar
Senior editor Hazel Egerton
Senior art editor Jacquie Gulliver
Production Ruth Cobb
Editorial consultant Angela Thomas
Picture research Giselle Harvey

First published in Great Britain in 1995
by Dorling Kindersley Limited
9 Henrietta Street, Covent Garden, London WC2E 8PS

A CIP catalogue record for this book is available from
the British Library.

ISBN 0 7513 3034 5

Colour reproduction by Colourscan, Singapore
Printed and bound in Italy by L.E.G.O.

CONTENTS

How to use this book

These pages show you how to use *Pockets: Ancient Egypt*. The book is divided into a number of sections, which cover different aspects of ancient Egyptian life. At the back of the book is a useful reference section. Each new section begins with a page that lists its contents.

EGYPTIAN LIFE
Ancient Egypt has been divided into subject areas and arranged in six main sections. In addition, there is an introductory section, which sets the scene by providing you with an overview of the subject, together with a brief history.

CORNER CODING
The corners of every page in the main section are colour coded to remind you which section you are in.

EGYPTIAN SOCIETY

LIFE IN ANCIENT EGYPT

GAMES AND LEISURE

BUILDING AND TECHNOLOGY

RELIGION

THE END OF AN ERA

HEADING
This describes the subject of the page. This page is about skills and artistry. If a subject continues over several pages, then the same heading applies.

INTRODUCTION
This provides a clear, general overview of the subject. After reading the introduction, you should have a good idea what the pages are about.

Heading Running head
Corner coding
Introduction

BUILDING AND TECHNOLOGY

SKILLS AND ARTISTRY

THE ANCIENT EGYPTIANS were very practical people. The great pyramids, tombs, and tem that still stand today show how they had ma many architectural and engineering problems. These monuments were and decorated by teams of skilled craftsmen, who worked year round for the pharaoh.

PLUMB LINE
Tools like this were used to make sure lines were vertical and to create grids for painting and carving on walls.

MUD BRICK

USING A MOULD
Wooden tomb models show of ancient Egyptians at work man is busy moulding a mud

Wood joins hold mould together

WOODEN BRICK MOULD

Handle

TECHNOLOGY F
• Pharaoh Khu had 23 life-size statues of himself for just one temp
• The first strike recorded history staged by craftsm working in the to Ramses III in 11
• The new capit Amarna was the planned city in t

MUD BRICK AND BRICK MOULD
The Egyptians built most of their buildings with bricks. Workmen used moulds like this to shape a mixture of Nile mud, sand, and straw. Bricks were not fired, just left to dry in the hot sun.

8 0

Fact bo

Label

LABELS
For extra clarity, some pictures have labels. They may give extra information, or identify a picture when it is not obvious from the text what the picture actually is.

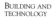

RUNNING HEADS

The running heads at the top of each page remind you which section you are in. The top of the left-hand page tells you the name of the section, and the top of the right-hand page tells you what the subject is about. The subject here is Skills and Artistry and it is in the Building and Technology section.

CAPTIONS AND ANNOTATIONS

Every illustration on a page has a caption. Each caption will go into a specific area of a subject. In addition to captions, there may also be annotations. These are in *italics* and draw your attention to particular features of an illustration. Annotations usually have leader lines.

Caption

ARCHITECTURE
THE SURVIVING buildings of ancient Egypt are mostly religious, either temples

SKILLS AND ARTISTRY

BEADWORK NECKLACE
Workshops produced jewellery for daily wear and for the tomb. The pharaoh sometimes ordered expensive pieces to mark special occasions or to give to foreign visitors. This funerary necklace was made c.330 B.C. The intricate beadwork incorporates tiny charms called amulets.

Hawk heads represent Horus

COLONNADE
Long colonnades were a feature of many temples. This one with palm-tree capitals is from Philae.

ARTISTIC LICENCE
Some of the highly elaborate architectural forms depicted in tomb paintings were obviously exaggerated.

Optional bud

Decorated with images of gods

CAPITAL FROM THE TEMPLE AT LUXOR

COLUMN
Temple columns could be fluted or smooth. But most were sculpted, often with elaborate reliefs that were then painted.

HIGH GATEWAY (MEDINET HABU)
Ramses III's mortuary temple and palace are enclosed within massive, 10 m (33 ft) thick walls. This monumental gateway was the main entrance to this Theban complex.

Window

KING'S HAREEM
Some of the rooms in the three-storey gateway were used as a hareem. Walls show scenes of Ramses III being attended by young women.

Detail from the painted pavement in Akhenaten's palace

FLOOR FRESCOES
The walls and floors of palaces and villas were plastered and painted with bright frescoes of patterns or nature scenes. These are from Akhenaten's palace.

AKHENATEN'S PALACE AT AMARNA
Nothing but raised foundations of this palace remain. But it can be imagined from paintings in the tomb of high priest Meryre. This reconstructed storage area was just a small part of the vast palace complex, which was set amongst landscaped gardens with many trees and shady pools.

Bes, a deity who warded off evil

Palette of pens

Stone hammer

Pectoral

Chisel

ART
...e of the greatest art ...de for the tombs ...s and nobles. On ...oden funerary stela, ...ess raises her hands ...ation of Ra-Horakhty ...con-headed sun god.

Three-legged stool *Ebony casket* *Engraving metal vessel* *Goldsmith finishing sphinx*

METALWORK
There are many paintings of craft workshops. In this detail, two jewellers finish a pectoral (pendant) and place it in a casket. To the right, a man engraves an inscription, while another is working on a golden sphinx. Other scenes in the same tomb show controllers weighing gold and checking finished articles. In reality, this workshop must have been noisy, dirty, and very hot.

REFERENCE SECTION

The reference section pages are yellow and appear at the back of the book. On these, you will find useful facts, dates, and charts. This section includes maps showing ancient sites, a list of dynasties, famous pharaohs, and a feature on reading and writing hieroglyphs.

Annotation

FACT BOXES

The introductory pages to each section and sub-section have fact boxes. These boxes contain interesting, at-a-glance information about the subject covered in that section.

GLOSSARY AND INDEX

There is a glossary and an index at the back of the book. The glossary defines and explains words and terms in this book that are specific to ancient Egyptian life. The index lists every subject alphabetically.

INTRODUCTION TO ANCIENT EGYPT

EGYPT TODAY

THE RIVER NILE and the Sahara Desert dominate Egypt. Until recently, the Nile flooded every year, bringing fertile black soil to the farmland on its banks. The ancient Egyptians called this lush strip the "black land", the land of life. The scorching desert was the "red land", the land of death.

CAIRO
Egypt's capital, Cairo, is the largest city in Africa, with a population of over 11 million. It was founded by Muslims in A.D. 969, more than a thousand years after the last pharaoh.

SAILING ON THE NILE
The Nile is the longest river in the world, flowing 6,670 km (4,145 miles) from the highlands of East Africa to the Mediterranean Sea.

FACTS ABOUT EGYPT

• The Sahara is the world's largest desert.

• Egypt is Africa's second biggest country (population: 55 million).

• Egypt has been a Muslim country since A.D. 642.

• The Aswan High Dam, built in 1969-70, ended the annual floods.

PYRAMIDS AND SPHINX
These famous monuments are both in Giza, on the outskirts of Cairo. They were built 4,500 years ago, during the period known as the Old Kingdom.

QUEEN HATSHEPSUT'S TEMPLE
Millions of tourists come to
Egypt every year to visit its great
monuments and museums. This
is Queen Hatshepsut's mortuary
temple at Deir el-Bahri on the
west bank of the Nile near Luxor.

KING'S COFFIN
The Egyptians had
elaborate beliefs
about life after
death. Pharaohs
and the elite were
mummified and
buried with a
wealth of treasure
in decorated
tombs. These
are a rich source
of information
on ancient life.

MODERN MAP WITH OLD SITES
Build-ups of silt in the north
has altered Egypt's coastline.
Other changes are the Suez
Canal and Aswan Dam.

THE RIVER NILE

EGYPT HAS BEEN CALLED "the Gift of the Nile". All the water for drinking, bathing, and watering crops came from the great river. The Nile was also Egypt's main highway. The dominant wind blew from north to south, so boats could float downstream with the current or sail upstream against it.

ANCIENT WAYS
Egyptians still grow crops and raise livestock on the banks of the Nile, as they have been doing for more than 7,000 years.

Sun canopy

Steersman

Steerin oar

TOMB MODEL FOR USE IN THE AFTERLIFE

Man rowing

FISHING NET

Prow

FISH HOOKS

BOAT
A text from c.1100 B.C. records "Merchants sail up and downstream, eager to convey goods from one place to another and to supply whatever is needed anywhere".

HUNTING AND FISHING
The Nile teemed with life. Men hunted birds in the marshes and caught fish with nets or hooks and lines. Children were taught to be afraid of crocodiles and hippos, which could overturn boats.

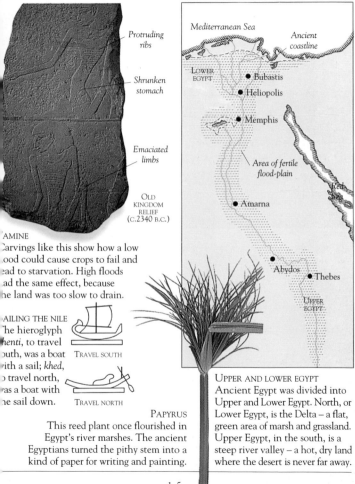

Protruding
ribs

Shrunken
stomach

Emaciated
limbs

OLD
KINGDOM
RELIEF
(C.2340 B.C.)

Mediterranean Sea

Ancient
coastline

LOWER
EGYPT

● Bubastis

● Heliopolis

● Memphis

Area of fertile
flood-plain

Red
Sea

● Amarna

Abydos ● ● Thebes

UPPER
EGYPT

FAMINE
Carvings like this show how a low
flood could cause crops to fail and
lead to starvation. High floods
had the same effect, because
the land was too slow to drain.

SAILING THE NILE
The hieroglyph
khenti, to travel
south, was a boat
with a sail; *khed*,
to travel north,
was a boat with
the sail down.

TRAVEL SOUTH

TRAVEL NORTH

PAPYRUS
This reed plant once flourished in
Egypt's river marshes. The ancient
Egyptians turned the pithy stem into a
kind of paper for writing and painting.

UPPER AND LOWER EGYPT
Ancient Egypt was divided into
Upper and Lower Egypt. North, or
Lower Egypt, is the Delta – a flat,
green area of marsh and grassland.
Upper Egypt, in the south, is a
steep river valley – a hot, dry land
where the desert is never far away.

THE SOURCES

OUR KNOWLEDGE of ancient Egypt comes
from buildings, objects, and writings.
Many disappeared over the centuries.
Thieves stole treasures, and the desert
sands invaded temples and tombs. But a
hot, dry climate preserved monuments
well. Egyptologists study these, and
other sources, for clues to Egypt's past.

MYSTERIOUS LAND
Sources can never give
a complete picture of the
past. This is the Queen of
Punt, a land somewhere
to the south. We still do
not know exactly where.

GUTENBERG BIBLE
Jews and Christians learned
about Egypt from the Old
Testament of the Bible (the
Jewish Torah). It tells the
story of the Jews' exile in
Egypt, where many worked
as slaves for the pharaoh.

THE FIRST PRINTED BIBLE

*The body
is coated
head to toe
in resin*

NAPOLEON IN EGYPT

When the French general Napoleon invaded Egypt in 1798, he brought a team of scholars and artists who made detailed studies of temples, tombs, and mummies. This sparked off the West's fascination with Egypt.

An owl stood for "m"   *"Mouth" or "r"*   *Bandages*

HIEROGLYPHS

Egyptian monuments, statues, and other artefacts are covered in hieroglyphs, a type of picture-writing. In 1822, French linguist Champollion discovered how to read them and opened up a huge new source of information.

Mummy case
Skeleton

MUMMY SCAN

During the 19th century, mummies were unwrapped, often as public events. This was destructive and disrespectful. Now modern scanners can create 3-D X-ray images of a mummy.

Linen bandages

MUMMIFICATION

The Egyptians went to incredible lengths to preserve their bodies for eternity. Mummies give us all sorts of information about health, diet, and disease. This woman's teeth were worn down by a lifetime of chewing coarse bread. We can even identify the plant oils used to preserve her skin.

BEFORE THE PHARAOHS

SETTLERS BEGAN TO FARM the Nile
Valley in about 5000 B.C. They
prospered and eventually formed
two kingdoms, Upper Egypt
and Lower Egypt. These early
Egyptians believed in life after
death. They buried their
dead in sand graves with
items for the next life.

NECKLACE
Sand graves have
revealed many items
of personal adornment,
such as jewellery of beads
and shells. This ancient
necklace is threaded
with semi-precious
stones from the
desert.

— Carnelian

FLINT KNIFE
In this period, the Egyptians were already
skilled stoneworkers. They carved elegant
ceremonial knives and daggers. The flint blades
were set in handles made from
bone or ivory.

Blade is
delicately
curved

Roofs
were
thatched

Wattle and
daub walls

Wood
beams above
doors and windows

MODEL HOUSE FROM GRAVE
The time before the pharaohs is known as the
Predynastic period (5000-3100 B.C.). In Upper
Egypt, farmers lived in small villages on the high
ground above the Nile, in houses like this.

Toenail

Zigzag patterns on backs of hippos

Inlaid eyes

FAIENCE BABOON
This is made from a glazed earthenware called faience, which first appeared in Egypt during this period.

HIPPO BOWL
Early potters used Nile silt and clay. The river was also a source of inspiration. This bowl is decorated with hippos.

SHEEP SHAPE
This sheep-shaped stone palette was for grinding make-up. Others are in the form of hippos, turtles, and falcons. These mysterious objects probably had a magical purpose as well.

Dry skin

Hair

Bodies were buried facing west to the setting sun

Knees pulled up against chest

GINGERELLA
She died 5,000 years ago. But this Egyptian woman's hair, skin, and nails have been remarkably well preserved by the hot desert sands. She has been nicknamed Gingerella because of her red hair.

THE OLD KINGDOM

EGYPT WAS UNIFIED for the first time in about 3100 B.C., more than 400 years before the start of the Old Kingdom, or "Pyramid Age". Under the stable rule of powerful pharaohs, the country's economy and culture flourished. Art and architecture reached a peak with the building of the great pyramids at Giza.

DOUBLE CROWN
As a symbol of his power, the pharaoh wore the *pschent* or double crown. This combined the White Crown, worn by the kings of Upper Egypt, and the Red Crown of Lower Egypt's kings

RULER OF TWO LANDS
The union of Egypt is shown here by the entwined lotus (symbol of Upper Egypt) and papyrus (Lower Egypt). One of the pharaoh's official titles was "Ruler of the Two Lands".

Painted limestone

Papyrus plant

Lotus

KING KHAFRA'S THRONE (DETAIL)

ROYAL COUPLE
These beautiful statues are Prince Rahotep and his wife Nofret. They were found near the pyramid of his father, King Sneferu. The statues are so lifelike it is hard to believe they are 4,600 years old. The eyes are rock crystal, with irises of purple amethyst.

FIRST PHARAOH?
Legend tells that
Egypt was united
by Menes, a king
from Upper Egypt
who conquered
the north. Experts
believe he may be
King Narmer (here
wearing the White
Crown). On the other
side of this palette, he
wears the Red Crown.

NARMER'S
PALETTE

King
Narmer

STEP PYRAMID
The first pyramid was built
at Saqqara for King Djoser in
c.2680 B.C. This huge stepped
structure is 60 m (198 ft) high.
Like most pyramids, it is a tomb.
Djoser and his family were
buried in chambers far beneath.

KHUFU
SMITES
ENEMY
CHIEF

MIGHTY KINGS
Kings Khufu, Khafra, and
Menkaura, builders of the
Pyramids of Giza, were
among the most powerful.
They must have directed
Egypt's entire economy
into building their tombs.

Nemes
headdress

Sky god,
Horus

Royal beard

GOD-KING
The Egyptians believed
that the pharaoh was the
son of the sun god Ra. The
king was also associated with the
sky god, Horus, seen here as a
falcon protecting Khafra.

2 1

THE MIDDLE KINGDOM

THE OLD KINGDOM COLLAPSED in about 2160 B.C., and Egypt was rocked by war and chaos. It was eventually reunited by Mentuhotep, who founded the Middle Kingdom in 2040 B.C. Peace and prosperity returned. Strong pharaohs strengthened government and foreign trade, and Egypt invaded Libya and Nubia. Art revived, and pyramids were built again.

SENUSRET I
This dynamic king took the throne after sharing it for ten years with his father, Amenemhat I. Senusret I fought the Libyans and Nubians and built many grand temples. The earliest known literary texts were written in his court.

ETERNAL STONE
This noble died in abo 1850 B.C. Statues like this were placed in loc temples, so relatives d not have to travel to tomb with offerings.

Spells cover coffin inside and out

MUMMY CASE
Middle Kingdom coffins were painted with magical spells to help the soul on its journey through the underworld to the next life. During the Old Kingdom, these spells – known as the Pyramid texts – had been carved in royal tombs.

BLACK PYRAMID
This is the first pyramid of Amenemhat III, which he built at Dahshur. Like all Middle Kingdom pyramids, the core is of mud bricks rather than stone. These have collapsed in a shapeless heap.

AMENEMHAT III
During his long and peaceful reign (1854-1808 B.C.) this powerful pharaoh built temples, border forts, two pyramids, and undertook a land reclamation scheme.

UNDER THE BLACK PYRAMID
Kings built mazes of false passages and hidden doors to try to conceal their burial chambers from robbers. It did not work. The Middle Kingdom collapsed in 1750 B.C., and all the pyramids were looted during the chaos that followed.

Pyramid enclosure wall

Extent of rubble

King's burial chamber

Entrance

False eyes allow mummy to "see" out

OSIRIS

GOD OF THE DEAD
The worship of Osiris, god of death and rebirth, spread across Egypt in the Middle Kingdom. He offered all Egyptians, not just those close to the pharaoh, the hope of an afterlife.

THE NEW KINGDOM

THE GREATEST PERIOD of Egypt's history was the New Kingdom (c.1550-1086 B.C.). Warrior kings, such as Ahmose I and Thutmose III, expanded the empire into Nubia, Libya, and the Middle East. Many temples were built, and pharaohs were buried in painted tombs in the Valley of the Kings.

WAR CROWN
The pharaoh's new image was as a war leader. He adopted the Blue Crown, or war helmet, and was seen as a living form of a warrior god.

UNFINISHED BUST OF AKHENATEN

RAMSES THE GREAT
In his 67 years on the throne, Ramses II built more monuments than any other pharaoh. This is the massive rock-cut temple of Abu Simbel. The four statues of Ramses II are each 20 m (65 ft) high

AKHENATEN, HERETIC PHARAOH
Pharaoh Amenhotep IV introduced a new religion, the first in history based on the worship of one god (the Aten). He even changed his name to Akhenaten. After his death, his name was scorned, his city abandoned, and the gods were reinstated

WAR CHARIOT
To expel Asian invaders,
the first pharaohs of
the New Kingdom built an
efficient army. This included corps of war
chariots, copied from the Asian enemy.

MASS GLASS
Factories, mass-producing
colourful glass vessels, were
set up near many palaces.
Glass was also cast to
decorate jewellery, furniture,
and even mummy cases.

TOMB OF SENNEDJEM (DEIR EL-MEDINA)
The Egyptians gave up on pyramid tombs, which were
too easy to find and rob. Instead, they were buried in
tombs cut deep into the rock in barren spots like the
Valley of the Kings and the Valley of the Queens.

TUTANKHAMUN'S SECOND COFFIN
The tombs in the Valley of the Kings were robbed long ago.
The only one found intact belonged to an obscure boy-king
called Tutankhamun. The glittering treasures
inside amazed the world.

Coloured
glass

EGYPTIAN SOCIETY

THE PEOPLE OF EGYPT

AT THE TOP of Egyptian society was the pharaoh. He commanded the army and ruled the country through a network of nobles, officials, and scribes. Skillful craftsworkers were kept busy building and decorating temples and tombs. But most Egyptians were peasant who worked the land.

AT THE PHARAOH'S SIDE
In life as in death, the king was surrounded by his nobles. This noble's tomb is in the shadow of King Khufu' Pyramid.

Tomb of Seshemnufer

SERVANT GIRL
Many women worked as servants in the houses of the rich. This wooden palette is in the shape of a serving girl, carrying a large pot on one shoulder. It is a make-up container; the top slides open and closed.

A KEEPER OF RECORDS
Scribes were important because they were among the few who could read and write. They recorded many details of everyday life.

FACTS ABOUT PEOPLE

• A massive tomb recently discovered in the Valley of the Kings (1995) shows that it contains at least some of Ramses II's many sons.

• When the pharaoh praised one man's work, the man died of shock.

HARVEST SCENE
Farming life followed the seasons. As soon as the summer's crop was ripe, farmers rushed to harvest it before the Nile flooded the land again. These oxen are treading the grain.

OFFICIAL
The state was highly bureaucratic. Every town had officials. These civil servants collected taxes, regulated businesses, and organized loans and marriage contracts.

CRAFTSMEN
Most craftsmen were employed in workshops run by royal palaces or temples. This carpenter is building a ship for a wealthy patron.

MUSICIAN
The Egyptians believed in enjoying life. Dancers and musicians performed at the royal courts and at private dinner parties. They also entertained the bustling crowds during festivals and celebrations.

KING AND CAPTIVE
The pharaoh was seen as a living god. He led in battle and protected Egypt from famine, disease, and chaos. This is symbolized by this statue of pharaoh Ramses IV gripping a captive enemy.

29

PEASANTS AND SERVANTS

THE VAST MAJORITY of ancient Egyptians were peasant farmers. They worked in the fields by the Nile, channelling the floodwaters and planting and harvesting crops. Many others worked as servants or labourers. Few of them could read or write. But they enjoyed more freedom than slaves, who were rare.

FOREIGN SLAVES
Slaves were never an important part of Egyptian society and were rare until the New Kingdom. Most slaves were foreigners, captured during Egypt's wars abroad. Here, a scribe registers foreign captives.

Man climbs stairs to roof terrace

Chest

Low bed

A WORKER'S HOME
The homes of the lower classes were small and cramped. The people spent most of their time up on the roof terrace or cooking in the court. In winter, a fire warmed the room, and the air was thick with smoke.

Cooking was done outdoors

Mud brick wall

A BEATING
Peasants who did not pay their taxes were beaten. More serious criminals were whipped or had their noses cut off and then sent to the mines of Sinai or Nubia.

GRAPE PICKING
Harvest time was very busy. These men are picking grapes and carrying them in buckets to the press. The squeezed juice was turned into wine.

TRAMPLED UNDER FOOT
These bound Libyans, painted on the soles of shoes, symbolized Egypt's power over foreigners. Slaves could be bought and sold like cattle, but they could also rent land and earn their freedom.

SERVANT GIRL
Most domestic servants were just poor. But some were female slaves who had escaped debt by selling themselves into slavery. The purchaser agreed to protect and feed the slave – and might later free her.

Quern (grind stone)

WOODEN MODEL OF SERVANT GRINDING CORN

MODEL WORKER
Egyptians believed that, in heaven, they would work for the gods in the *Field of Reeds*. The rich were buried with model *shabti* figures, to do the hard work for them.

MIDDLE CLASSES

EGYPT'S EFFICIENT administration
was run by an educated middle
class of scribes and officials. Military
officers ran the army, while priests
organized prayers and offerings in the
temples. Lower on the social pyramid
were craftsworkers and traders – but
they still had a much better standard
of living than the peasant farmers.

ARTISANS
Jewellers present finished
works to their workshop
supervisor. Craftsmen
worked long hours in
hot, dirty conditions and
were given little personal
credit for the beautiful
works of art they produced

MEDICAL DOCTOR
This is one of just two known images
of a doctor at work. Many priests
and scribes were also doctors. Some
specialized in treating the eyes, teeth,
or the head. One priest had the
title "Doctor to the King's Belly".

*A variety
of trees*

Sistrum
(*ceremonial rattle*)

Incense
cone

*The garden pool
would have
been stocked
with fish*

PRIEST
In countless temples throughout the land, teams of priests and priestesses made offerings to the gods in the name of their pharaoh. In return, they were rewarded with land and a generous income.

Shrine of god Atum

Papyrus

Vents to catch cool breeze

SERVANT
Well-off middle-class families had servants to cook, clean, and help them wash and dress. This servant is placing an incense cone on his master's head, ready for a night out.

This official carries a wooden staff, which was a symbol of authority

SCRIBE
In most towns and villages, the only people who could read and write were scribes, which made them powerful and influential people. Art often shows them sitting cross-legged. This scribe is Pes-shu-per, c.700 B.C.

WELL-TO-DO COUPLE
This detail from a papyrus shows the scribe Nakhte and his wife in the garden of their villa. A platform protects the house from high floodwaters. The couple are wearing elaborately pleated clothes and heavy wigs.

OFFICIAL
The government was run by state officials, ranging from the *Vizier*, the top statesman, to local officials who ran the day-to-day affairs in each district, or *nome*.

THE ARMY

EGYPT'S FIGHTING forces evolved from the Old Kingdom tradition of mustering troops when an emergency arose to the large, well-equipped army of the New Kingdom. In supreme control was the pharaoh. Below him, ranking officers commanded corps of soldiers, who fought on foot or in chariots.

WAR GALLEY
Armed with axes and bows, the navy fought sea battles from ships. These had figureheads of gods and names like "Wild Bull", "Star of Egypt", or "Soul of the Gods".

STING OF BATTLE
The pharaoh thanked soldiers for bravery in battle by giving them gold flies, made in the royal workshops by the best jewellers. Worn around the neck, the fly meant that a soldier had "stung" the enemy.

BATTLE FORMATION
In the periods of disorder that followed the Old Kingdom's collapse, many regional princes owned armies. This model, c.2000 B.C., from the tomb of Prince Mesehti may represent his private army.

STANDARD TACTICS
The pharaoh and his council of war decided on strategy. Every unit of the Egyptian army carried a standard so that they were easy to identify on the battle field. Orders were given by war trumpet.

PEACE WORK

In peacetime, the army was
put to work digging ditches,
mining, or hauling stone
for temples and pyramids.
The navy went on trading
expeditions. This wall carving
from Queen Hatshepsut's temple
shows a trip, c.1496 B.C., to the
Land of Punt. The fleet returned
with baboons and incense trees.

Domed
houses
on stilts

Many different
trees and
plants

BORDER FORT

During the Middle Kingdom, massive mud-brick
forts were built to protect Egypt's border with Nubia.
Egyptian art never shows these forts under seige.

FORCED MARCH

Many soldiers were recruited by
force. They were sent to boot camp,
where their hair was cut and they
were taught to use their weapons.

WRITING IT ALL DOWN

Army scribes kept all records of
recruits, stores, weapons, and pay.
Many scribes became officers and
went on to join the general staff,
where battle tactics were decided.

Papyrus
scroll

EGYPTIAN WOMEN

WOMEN HAD CLEARLY DEFINED roles. They were responsible for looking after the house and bringing up the children. Many did a lot of back-breaking labour, such as working in the fields. But, by law, women had the same rights as men. A wife could even take her husband to court if he treated her badly.

A DELAYED BEATING
Egyptian criminals were beaten. But an exception was made with pregnant women, so as not to hurt the innocent unborn child. Punishment had to wait until after the birth.

Coffins fit inside each other

BRINGING UP BABY
A woman's main job was raising children. Mothers carried babies in slings. If a wife did not bear a son, her husband would take a mistress, and the family would adopt the child.

GOLDEN PRIESTESS
"Priestess" was one of the few titles women could have. Another was "Player of Music in the Temple". These golden coffins belong to Henutmehit, a priestess of the city of Thebes, c.1250 B.C.

MARRIED COUPLE

This happy-looking couple are Katep and his wife Hetepheres, c.2500 B.C. Some unions were arranged, but other Egyptians married for love. Men could have several wives, but the marriage contract protected the wife and children, so most men could only afford one.

Woman's pale skin suggests she stayed in the home

BREAST MILK JUG

Mothers breastfed their babies openly. One carving even shows Queen Nefertiti nursing her daughter. Excess milk may have been kept in jugs like this. Mothers with a short supply prayed to the goddess Isis.

Woman carries basket on head

Base fitted in stand

NEFERTITI

This statue of the beloved wife of king Akhenaten was found in a sculptor's workshop in Amarna. After her husband's death Nefertiti may even have ruled on her own under a false name.

Face of Hatshepsut

A WOMAN KING

Hatshepsut was the first woman to become a true pharaoh (1479-1457 B.C.). Like other pharaohs, Hatshepsut had herself portrayed as a sphinx.

Ceremonial beard

WOMAN'S WORK

Many women were household servants. Others worked as wet nurses, bakers, weavers, singers, dancers, musicians, and even doctors. But women never held public office.

THE PHARAOH

EGYPTIANS BELIEVED their pharaoh was a living god. He alone could unite the country and maintain the cosmic order, or *Ma'at*. They believed that, when he died, he would achieve eternal life – not just for himself, but also for his people. The pharaoh's power was absolute. He led the army, set taxes, judged criminals, and controlled the temples.

HORUS
The pharaoh was associated with the gods of the sun and sky, especially the falcon-headed sky god Horus.

Thutmose IV

ROYAL NAME
A pharaoh's name was written inside a cartouche. This oval loop symbolized the king's power over "all that the sun encircles".

KING OF THE NILE
Hapy was the god of the Nile flood. He was portrayed as a king, wearing the royal *nemes* headdress and false beard. The woman's breasts were symbolic of his waters, which gave life to Egypt.

ANKH
The ankh was the symbol of life. In art, only gods or kings carry this symbol. Many paintings show a god or goddess giving life to a pharaoh by touching his mouth with the ankh.

SYMBOLS OF THE PHARAOH
Tutankhamun carries a crook and flail and wears the striped *nemes* headcloth and ceremonial beard. The vulture and cobra on his brow represent Upper and Lower Egypt, respectively.

The Uraeus (said to spit fire at the king's enemies)

Vulture goddess Nekhbet

Nemes headcloth

PEPY II
This pharaoh ruled for 94 years. Every 30 years the pharaoh was recrowned in the *Sed* festival, a jubilee celebration. The highlight was a race in which the king ran a course to prove his fitness to rule.

False beard

OSTRICH-FEATHER FAN
The pharaoh was almighty. Servants fanned him, and visitors kissed the ground before him. But anyone touching him without permission could be sentenced to death.

Crook

THE ROYAL HOUSE

IMPORTANT OFFICIALS were called "Friends of the Pharaoh". They had titles like "Fanbearer on the Right of the King" and "Master of the Horse". Many of them lived at the palace. On great state occasions, they would be joined by high priests and officials from all over Egypt.

ROYAL SPORT
The sport of kings and their courts was hunting. Noblemen killed birds with throwing sticks. The cartouche of pharaoh Akhenaten is painted on this fragile example, which was probably only ever used for ceremonial purposes.

18TH DYNASTY THRONE

RAMSES III AND HAREM
The pharaoh lived in a harem, a court of many wives and other women. They washed and dressed him many times a day and catered to his every need.

POWER OF THE THRONE
The pharaoh's might was visible throughout the palace. This throne has bound captives under the seat, showing the king's control over foreigners and his role as defender of Egypt.

TUTANKHAMUN'S OFFICIALS
A painting in Tutankhamun's tomb shows the court officials dragging the king's coffin at his funeral. In his lifetime, they would have helped the king in the day-to-day affairs of state.

PREGNANT QUEEN
This is the only known image of a pregnant queen. She is the mother of King Thutmose III. One king could have many wives. To keep the dynastic line pure, pharaohs often married their sisters and cousins – and sometimes even their own daughters.

A PRINCE
It was very important for the pharaoh to have an heir. If his chief wife had no sons, a boy born by one of his other wives became heir. If he had no sons, the next pharaoh could start a new dynasty.

RAMESSIDE QUEEN

COURT OFFICIAL
This is Sennefer and his wife. He was "Prince of the Southern City" (Thebes) and "Administrator of Granaries" in c.1400 B.C. Sennefer's wife was a royal wet-nurse.

GODDESS QUEEN
The pharaoh's chief wife ruled beside him as his queen. She was also looked upon as a god on earth. The king represented the all-powerful sun god, while she was associated with Hathor, goddess of love, and Isis, the mother goddess.

4 1

LIFE IN ANCIENT EGYPT

EVERYDAY LIFE

EGYPTIAN LIFE revolved around three seasons. During the flood, *akhet* (July to October), farm work stopped. *Peret*, the time of ploughing and sowing, began when the waters went down in November. The busiest season was *shemu*, the harvest. From March to June, farmers worked hard to bring in the crops before the river rose again.

IRRIGATION DEVICE
Farmers used *shadufs* to raise water from the river. They irrigated the land by using a system of canals and dykes.

PYRAMID
Thousands of farmers had nothing to do during the flood season. So they joined the pharaoh's skilled labour force to work on huge building projects like temples or pyramids. This is the remains of the Meidum pyramid, built around 2550 B.C. for the pharaoh Sneferu.

Limestone core of pyramid

Farmland on edge of desert

HUNTING IN THE MARSHES
Work and play centred on the Nile. This tomb carving shows cattle being herded across the river. The calf being helped into a boat is about to be grabbed by a crocodile.

In the Old Kingdom, silver was far rarer than gold

THE SIDELOCK OF YOUTH
Children often ran around naked in the hot climate. They are usually shown with a distinctive hairstyle.

RINGS
Both men and women enjoyed wearing jewellery, which was often made from precious metals. These swivel-top rings have scarab beetles one side and good-luck designs the other.

CATTLE COUNT
This wooden model shows the cattle count, an event that took place every year or so. This was a means of assessing a person's wealth. The cattle are driven past scribes, who write down the numbers for the owner's tax records.

ANIMALS OF THE NILE

IN ANCIENT TIMES, a great variety of animals thrived in Egypt. The desert was home to lions, wolves, antelopes, wild bulls, and hares. The river marshes echoed with the loud cries of exotic birds. Crocodiles lazed on the banks, while hippos wallowed in the water. At night, owls, jackals, and hyenas came out in search of food.

CAT MUMMY
Sacred to the goddess Bastet, cats were popular pets. Cats were often mummified and buried in cat-shaped coffins after they died.

CROCODILE GOD
Many people were killed by the huge Nile crocodiles. The anima was worshipped as the god Sobel

ANIMAL GAMES
This comical papyrus gives us a glimpse of ancient Egyptian humour. Like the lion and antelope playing senet, the animals are all doing things that are wildly out of character.

Senet was a popular board game

Mouth poured perfume *Ripples for scales*

FLASK
Fish such as perch and catfish were caught up and down the river. This fish-shaped glass flask poured perfume from its mouth.

WILD SHEEP
This figurine may once have graced the dressing table of a wealthy lady. It is a cosmetic container in the shape of a wild sheep, an animal that still roams the fringes of the Sahara today.

Lid of container

Crouching cat

Water-plant design

HIPPO
This animal was feared because it overturned boats. In legend, it was associated with the evil god Seth, so killing a hippo was a symbolic victory over evil. The wealthy hunted them with spears.

Jackals herd goats *A cat tends a flock of geese* *Lion and ox play*

FARMING

EGYPTIAN LIFE was based on farming th rich flood plain of the Nile. The mai crops were emmer wheat, barley, and flax. Farmers also grew beans, lentils, onions, leeks, cucumbers, and lettuce in garden plots, and fruits like grapes, dates, figs, and pomegranates. Animals raised for meat included cattle, pigs, sheep, goats, geese, and ducks.

PICKING FIGS
Ancient Egyptians loved sycamore figs. So did baboons, which were trained to climb the trees and pick the fruit.

Scribes making tax records

Wooden chest

Tomb owner

Man with j of water

Man drinking water from jar

Mother with baby

Workers cutting grain with sickles

Men carry grain in ba

PLOUGHING THE FIELDS
This wooden tomb model shows a man
ploughing. The wooden plough is being
pulled by two oxen. The ploughman used
a hoe if he needed to break up any heavy
clumps of soil. Another man would have
followed behind, sowing seed.

*Man guides
plough*

*The wooden blade
cuts through
the soil*

WATERING THE CROPS
A network of dykes, pools,
and irrigation channels
criss-crossed the farmland.
Here, a man is carrying
buckets of water hung on
a yoke across his
shoulders.

Workers winnowing

HARVESTING GRAIN
This is a harvesting scene from a tomb.
Below, workers cut the grain and load it
into baskets. Above, other workers are
winnowing – throwing the grain into
the air to separate it from the chaff.
Scribes record
the quantity.

*Protective
headcloth*

LENTILS

DATES

*Girls squabbling
about left-over wheat* *Linen
kilt*

WHEAT

CROPS
The fertile
soil by the Nile
enabled Egyptian
farmers to grow a
large variety of crops.
Harvested grain was
stored in granaries and
used to make bread and beer.

FOOD AND DRINK

BREAD AND BEER were the two staples in an Egyptian's diet. Both were made in a similar way, using wheat or barley. Bakers also made a whole variety of cakes and pastries, often sweetened with dates or honey. There were many fruits and vegetables, but potatoes and citrus fruits were unknown. The wealthy enjoyed lavish banquets – feasting on meat, washed down with wine. Poor people were more likely to dine on fish and beer.

HONEY
Egyptians were the first people known to keep bees. Honey was collected to sweeten cakes, beer, and wine.

Wooden syphon

BEER STRAINER

Holes for straining

GRAPES

GRAPES AND WINE
Wall-paintings show workers picking grapes and squeezing them in a press. The wine matured in tall amphorae, inscribed with the year, type of grape, region, and vineyard owner.

WINEPRESS

BREWING BEER
Women made beer. They mixed bread dough with yeast and left it to ferment in large vats. A few weeks later, they filtered the mash. The mature beer was seasoned with spices or dates. It was very thick and had to be strained before drinking.

FOOD OFFERINGS
Egyptians brought food to temples and tombs to make sure the gods and spirits of the dead were well fed. This tomb carving shows bearers bringing a selection of offerings.

EVERYDAY FARE
Fruit, vegetables, and grain were grown in plenty. The Egyptians ate bread with every meal. Until the New Kingdom, when bakeries became common, most housewives made their own bread. Loaves came in many shapes, some made specially for religious rites such as offerings for the dead. This bread was placed in a tomb more than 3,000 years ago.

Baboons could not resist figs

MODERN FIGS

BREAD

MODERN DATES

AT THE BUTCHERS
This tomb model shows an ox being slaughtered. The meat would be roasted, boiled, or stewed. Rich Egyptians ate a lot of meat, which was often wild game from the hunt. Antelope, gazelle, porcupine, hare, and fowl such as quail and crane were all on the menu.

ANCIENT PALM TREE FRUIT

EGGS FOR THE PHARAOH
Ostrich plumes and eggs were often among the tributes sent to pharaohs from lands in the south.

TRADE

FOR MOST OF ITS HISTORY, ancient Egypt was the richest country in the world. The Egyptians grew more than enough food. So the surplus grain, along with linen, papyrus, and dried fish, was exported in exchange for luxury items such as incense, silver, and fine cedar wood. Horses came from Asia to the east, while, to the south, Nubia and Punt were a source of gold, ivory, ebony, and incense.

Ebony

Red jasper

922

Incense

Gold rings

Giraffe tails

NUBIAN GIFTS
These Nubian envoys are taking gifts to the Egyptian court. Nubia was rich in copper, gold, and semi-precious stones. Merchants also supplied Egypt with exotic goods like incense and wild animals, brought from lands farther south.

Live baboon

KEY IMPORTS

- INCENSE
- SILVER
- TIMBER
- IVORY
- TURQUOISE
- LAPIS LAZULI
- HORSES
- GOLD
- EXOTIC ANIMALS

MAP OF MAIN IMPORTS
During various times, Egypt controlled the neighbouring lands of Palestine, Sinai, and Nubia and exploited their wealth.

Mediterranean Sea

WESTERN ASIA

SYRIA

PALESTINE

SINAI

Memphis

LIBYA

River Euphrates

Persian Gulf

River Nile

Thebes

EGYPT

Red Sea

NUBIA

TO PUNT

ARABIA

SAILING VESSEL
Most trade was done by ship. Vessels sailed up and down the Nile and the Mediterranean coast, transporting goods from place to place. Expeditions via the Red Sea to Punt (thought to be present-day Somalia) returned with cargoes of ivory, frankincense, and myrrh.

Square sail

Shallow bottom

MODEL OF BOAT C.1300 B.C.

5 3

EGYPTIAN HOUSING

EGYPTIAN HOMES were built to stay cool. From pharaoh's palace to worker's hut, most houses were made from mud bricks. Many dwellings had roof terraces, where people could take the air in hot weather. Wealthy families lived in large villas with lush gardens and fish-stocked pools. In the cities, the poorer people lived in simple homes, crammed together in a maze of alleys, passageways, and squares.

MAKING BRICKS
Wet Nile mud was mixed with sand and straw, squeezed into a wooden mould, and then dried in the sun.

ANCIENT FRESCOES
The walls and ceilings of rich people's houses were painted with colourful designs, often composed of geometric patterns and plant motifs.

The roof terrace was a cool place to sleep

Decorative pond

Kitchen area with open fire for cooking

INSIDE A HOUSE
In a typical house of a well-off Egyptian, the main living area was placed some way from the kitchen to avoid cooking smells. Some bedrooms had their own bathing facilities and lavatories.

Flat roof

Chair

Stairs to upper storey

Colonnaded entrance

Bed

Food was stored and cooked in courtyard

SIMPLE HOME
This pottery house (*c.*1900 B.C.) was placed in a tomb for the owner's use in the next life and shows architectural details that existed in houses of the period.

HOUSE FACTS

• Mud bricks were sometimes stamped with the name of the reigning pharaoh.

• A workman's week was nine days long – the 10th was a day of rest.

• Windows were small to keep out hot sunlight.

A VILLAGE ON THE NILE TODAY
Egyptian houses are still made of mud bricks. Some towns now sit on hills because they have been rebuilt again and again on the ruins of older settlements.

In the home

Egyptian houses were sparsely furnished. Tables were rare, and many pictures show people squatting cross-legged on the floor rather than sitting on stools. Most people slept on benches built into the walls; only the wealthy had real beds. The pieces of furniture that have survived have simple, elegant lines. Many are exquisitely crafted, with inlays of gemstones, glass, and precious woods.

NOBLE CHAIRS
Only a wealthy Egyptian household would have chairs. Like tables, these were usually low and wide Legs were often carved to look like lions' paws or bulls' hooves.

SERVANT LOOKING AFTER FIRE

Fanning flames

Special base holds jar steady

JAR STAND
Lamps and jars often sat on wooden stands. Oil lamps were the only means of artificial light. Oil was expensive, so many poorer people went to bed early and rose at dawn.

String

FIRE
This is the only type of Egyptian fire-making device found. A stick was pushed into a wooden base, while a bow looped around the stick was moved quickly back and forth. The friction set the base on fire.

Carved decoration

Bow

Painted legs

Firestick

End of stick fits into groove

Base

Grooves blackened by fire

LION HEAD
Walls and furniture were decorated with images of gods, especially ones that protected the household. This lion head may represent Bes, a guardian of sleep, who is half lion, half dwarf.

Cup in shape of open lotus

Ducks

CONTAINERS
The first vessels, from over 7,000 years ago, were clay pots. Later, carved stone jars were produced. Faience, a coloured and glazed earthenware, first appeared *c.*3200 B.C. This faience vase and cup from Thebes were made *c.*1450 B.C.

HEADRESTS
Instead of pillows, Egyptians slept on headrests. They were made from stone, wood, or bone. Much more comfortable than they look, headrests are still used in many parts of Africa.

Curved surface supports head

Wide base

String mesh netting

All six of Tutankhamun's beds have clawed feet

TUTANKHAMUN'S BED
Of the six beds discovered in Tutankhamun's tomb, this is the most spectacular. The carved ebony frame is completely covered in gold, and embossed panels are decorated with plant motifs. Another of his beds folded up for travelling.

CLOTHING

EGYPTIANS WORE simple linen clothes. Men dressed in short kilts, leaving their chests bare or draping a cloak or a strip of linen over their shoulders. Women wore long, tight-fitting dresses. On cool evenings they might put on a long-sleeved gown as well. In later periods, tunics and dresses with complicated pleats became popular. Both women and men wore wigs.

Damp cloth was pressed into grooves

PLEAT BOARD

PRESSED PLEATS
Grooved boards like this may have been used to pleat the clothes of well-to-do Egyptians.

COARSE LINEN
Ordinary Egyptians wore coarse linen, while the rich dressed in a lighter, finer cloth. Finest of all was the semi-transparent "royal linen". The Egyptians knew about dyes, but most linen was left a natural white.

Interwoven flax fibres

OFFICIAL ATTIRE
This is Mereruka, *vizier* to King Teti in about 2340 B.C. He is wearing the short kilt typical of the Old Kingdom. The kilt was tied at the waist, often in an elaborate bow.

ROYAL DRESS

Egyptians were not prudish about their bodies. Kings are often shown in tiny kilts, and queens wore near transparent dresses. For important ceremonies, the king wore a long kilt and an elaborate cloak with countless pleats.

COURT LADY

Clothes were draped rather than cut to fit. The fringed, finely pleated dress of this noblewoman leaves one shoulder bare and reaches well below her ankles. Her heavy, braided wig is crowned with a circlet of flowers.

WEAVING LINEN

Women combed the stems of the flax plant to remove the spiky heads. Then they separated the fibres from the stalk and spun them on a spindle, weighted by a whorl. The spun threads were woven on a loom to make cloth.

Whorl

FLAX COMB

SPINDLE

aTwine strap

DRESS FACTS

• Priests dressed statues of gods each morning and undressed them at night.

• Some peasants and fishermen worked naked.

• The wealthy used professional laundries. Poorer people did their washing in the river.

Rotating spindle twists fibres

SANDALS

Most Egyptians went barefoot. But priests and wealthy people wore sandals. These were made from leather or reeds like papyrus that flourished in the marshes by the River Nile.

Jewellery and make-up

The Egyptians went to great lengths to look good. Men and women rubbed oil into their skins, painted their eyes with thick make-up, and sprinkled their clothes with sweet-smelling perfumes. At parties, women crowned their wigs with incense cones. These melted slowly, pouring scent onto their hair and clothes. The wealthy wore gold jewellery that sparkled with semi-precious stones.

Malachite

Galena

COLOUR
Green eye paint came from malachite, black eye *kohl* from galena, and red for lips was made from iron oxide.

Iron oxide

EARRINGS

WIG FASHION
The Egyptians disliked body hair and shaved their heads and bodies with bronze razors. They wore wigs made from real human hair, curled or braided into many different shapes and styles.

Cowrie shell

Fish

Sidelock of youth

Heh, god of long life

Lotus flower

MAKE-UP POT
Many make-up pots are works of art. This one is made from the rare blue stone anhydrite.

Gold trim

GOLDEN GIRDLE
This is part of a piece of jewellery that was worn around the waist. It is strung with colourful beads of carnelian, amethyst, lapis lazuli, and turquoise, plus gold good-luck charm

COSMETIC PALETTE
This make-up container is carved
and painted to look like a bunch
of flowers. The buds are circles
of ivory, dyed a soft pink. The
swivelling top hides a hollow
where cosmetic cream was stored.

RACELET
Cobras protect the
ky god Horus on
his bracelet made
or a prince.

*Top swivels
sideways*

*Polished
metal surface*

*Lotus-style
headdress*

*Handle in
shape of
serving girl*

Duck

Leaves

METAL MIRROR
The Egyptians did
not have glass
mirrors. Instead,
they admired their
reflections in
polished discs of
copper or bronze.
The bright, shining
surfaces reminded
the Egyptians of the
sun they worshipped.

*Glass container
with applicator*

AKE-UP FOR EYES
ohl was kept in pots and applied
th thin metal tools. Even
ildren wore *kohl*, which also
otected against eye infections.

SCHOOLING AND WRITING

MOST EGYPTIAN CHILDREN did not go to school. To be a goldsmith or a painter, a boy trained in a workshop or with a team of workers building a tomb. Scribes were given a more formal education, starting at age nine and lasting about five years. They had to study hard and were beaten if they were lazy. But it was worth it – scribes were among the only people who could read or write, and this gave them status.

Layers placed at right angles

MAKING PAPYRUS
Paper was made from papyrus reed. The soft pith was cut into strips, placed in two layers, then pounded together to form a strong sheet.

Hieratic text always reads right to left

THREE SCRIPTS
Egyptian picture-writings are called hieroglyphs, the Greek word for "sacred carvings". Scribes later developed two other scripts, hieratic and demotic, which were much quicker to write.

Hieroglyphs read either left to right or right to left. They were written downwards in columns or in horizontal lines

When figures fa left, reader star on left-hand si

WRITING TOOLS

A scribe often had to travel on official business or to make tax assessments on distant farms. He took a water pot with him and reed brushes, pens, and ink, which fitted into a wooden case. He mixed his own ink, making black from soot or charcoal and colours from ground-up minerals. Reed pens were first used in Egypt during the Greek period.

Reed is split to hold ink

Brush holder, water pot, and palette

HIEROGLYPH FOR "SCRIBE" OR "WRITING"

Case with ink-well and pens

Papyrus scroll

SEATED SCRIBE
This scribe is shown in the traditional seated position. The sculptor has given him a chubby stomach. This is common in ancient Egyptian art, because obesity was regarded as a sign of success.

Deciphering hieroglyphs

For nearly 1,500 years, no one could read hieroglyphs, the ancient Egyptian picture-writing. The French scholar Jean-François Champollion spent most of his life trying to break the code. He made his first breakthrough in 1822, while studying the Rosetta Stone, and soon experts were able to read the inscriptions that cover many Egyptian artefacts.

The text is a message of thanks to Pharaoh Ptolemy V

Demotic

The loop represents eternity

ROYAL NAMES
A pharaoh's name was written inside an oval loop called a cartouche. This piece of jewellery contains the cartouche of Senusret II.

		~~	⊙	
Sa	Ankh	N	Ra	Nefer
Son	Life	Water	Day	Beautiful

PICTURES FOR WORDS AND SOUNDS
One hieroglyph can stand for either a word or a sound. For instance, a scribe would draw a goose both for the sound "sa" and the word "son".

A name of a pharaoh can be recognized because it is written within a cartouche

Hieroglyphs

JEAN-FRANÇOIS CHAMPOLLION (1790-1832)
A brilliant linguist, Champollion had mastered 12 languages by age 16. The first hieroglyphs he deciphered were pharaohs' names. By 1824, he had translated most of the symbols and begun to unravel Egyptian grammar.

"PTOLEMY" IN HIEROGLYPHS

"PTOLEMY" IN DEMOTIC

ΠΤΟΛΕΜΑΙΟΣ
"PTOLEMY" IN GREEK

THE ROSETTA STONE
Inscribed in 196 B.C., the Rosetta Stone was unearthed again in 1799. The text is repeated in hieroglyphs, demotic, and Greek. Champollion could read Greek, and so he used this text to translate the other two scripts.

CRACKING THE CODE
The English physicist Thomas Young was the first to recognize the hieroglyphs for Ptolemy and Cleopatra on the Rosetta Stone. But Champollion made the great breakthrough when he realized that some symbols stood for ideas while others were simply sounds.

P T O L M Y S

K L E O P A T R A

Greek

The Stone is a slab of black basalt, found near Rosetta in the delta

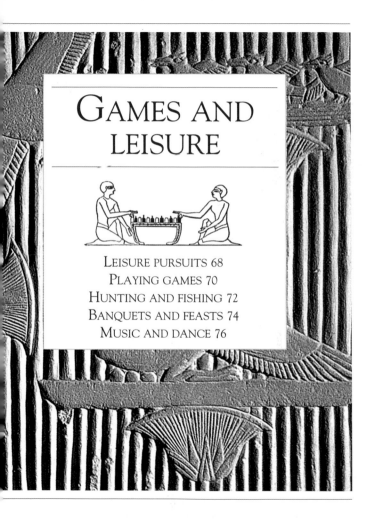

GAMES AND LEISURE

LEISURE PURSUITS

THE EGYPTIANS LIVED LIFE to the full. At public festivals and private parties they feasted and drank, entertained by singers, dancers, and musicians. Children played out in the sunshine, while adults revelled in sports like hunting and fishing. In quieter moments they wrote poetry or enjoyed board-games.

ANGLING
Egyptians were the first people to fish for pure pleasure. Nobles are often shown in armchairs, lazily dangling lines into their well-stocked garden pools.

ENTERTAINERS AT A BANQUET
Party scenes show how much the Egyptians liked music and dance. In this tomb painting, c.1400 B.C., one woman plays a double flute while others clap along or dance to the beat. In Egyptian art, it is very unusual to see faces front on.

LEISURE FACTS

• Egyptians swam backstroke and crawl. Upper-class children were given lessons.

• Farmworkers and fishermen had their own working songs.

• Festival revellers sailing on Nile barges sometimes "mooned" the crowd on the shore.

STONE THROWER
This is the earliest known example of a sling. It dates from about 1900 B.C. and was found in the town of Kahun in the Faiyum Oasis. The sling was probably used to scare birds away from Kahun's vineyards and lush gardens. One end of the cord was looped around a finger to keep hold of the sling after firing.

Woven cord

Loop for finger

FISHING IN THE MARSHES
These men are fishing from a reed boat. One man clubs the fish and puts them in a basket. Fish were sacred creatures in some areas and an important part of the diet in others. This even led to a war between neighbouring towns.

Carved gazelle head

Plain stick

THROW STICKS
Dice did not reach Egypt until the Greek era. Before then, players threw sticks like these. Each stick has a flat and a rounded side. The number of flat sides facing up probably determined a player's move.

Carved sticks may have had different values from plain sticks

ARCHERY PRACTICE
Men hunted with bows and arrows. During the New Kingdom, archers shot at prey while riding chariots. They practised archery by firing arrows at square targets made of copper. This drawing is copied from the Theban tomb of Min, a private man who taught archery to Amenhotep II.

Stones were loaded into this basket

Sling stones

PLAYING GAMES

IN THE WARM EGYPTIAN CLIMATE, boys and girls spent a lot of time outdoors, swimming, dancing, riding donkeys, and enjoying games of leapfrog and tug-of-war. They played with balls, dolls, toy animals, and pets such as cats, birds, and monkeys. The most popular board-game for adults was called senet. Tutankhamun liked it so much he was buried with four complete boards.

TOPS
Children spun these pottery tops with a twist of the fingers or a quick tug on a piece of string wrapped round the toy.

CLAY BALLS
Balls made of papyrus, cloth, and leather have all been found. These brightly painted clay balls were once filled with seeds or tiny lumps of clay to make them rattle when thrown.

String to move lower jaw

CAT TOY
Pulling the string on this carved wooden cat makes it open and close its mouth. Other ancient animal toys have glass eyes, movable legs and arms, and tails that wag.

CATCHING AND JUGGLING
This scene is copied from a Middle Kingdom tomb. These jugglers may have been professionals or people playing for fun or ritual.

HORSES AND MUMMIES

This wooden horse could be pulled along with a string through its nose. Nile mud animals, birds, and even tiny mummies lying in their coffins have been found. These may be toys made by children or votive offerings.

Wheel

Painted saddle

Senet

A GAME OF SENET

Senet was played by moving counters on a board of 30 squares – some were dangerous to land on, others were lucky. Unfortunately, the rules have been lost.

Fighting with wooden sticks

TOURNAMENTS

Men competed in games of boxing, wrestling, and fencing. King Ramses III held the first recorded fencing tournament in c.1250 B.C. Egyptian and allied soldiers fought with wooden sticks.

SNAKE GAME

This was one of the earliest Egyptian board-games. The playing surface is the shape of a coiled snake. Players started at the tip of the tail and tried to move balls towards the snake's head at the centre.

Winning position

Hieroglyph of pharaoh's name

HUNTING AND FISHING

THE MAIN SPORT for well-to-do Egyptians was hunting. In early times, nobles stalked antelope, bulls, and lions on foot; later they hunted from horse-drawn chariots. Pharaohs were proud of their kills. Amenhotep III boasted of 102 lions in ten years as king, and Thutmose III claimed 120 elephants during one trip to Syria.

MAN WITH ANTELOPE
A man returns from the hunt. Trained dogs or even hyenas were used to catch antelope or to chase them into traps.

HUNTING WITH NETS
Marsh hunters netted both fish and wild-fowl. They snared birds by baiting nets with corn or maggots.

FISHING FROM RAFTS
Egyptians fished for food and fun. During the Old Kingdom, fish were usually netted or speared. Later, angling became popular. The fishermen in this tomb relief are using hooks and nets to catch the fish.

*Papyrus
thicket*

*Throwing
stick*

Wife

*Duck
decoy*

*Daughter
steadies raft*

HUNTING HYENAS
Hyenas got into game reserves and were killed along with animals kept here as quarry. They were also hunted as a menace to domestic flocks.

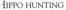

HIPPO HUNTING
These three men are spearing hippos from a papyrus raft. Spearheads were attached to long pieces of rope, so that the dying hippo could be hauled onto land.

FOWLING
Nobles preferred to hunt birds with a throwing stick. It was like a boomerang and killed a bird by breaking its neck. This man has brought his family, including pet cat, on the hunt.

BANQUETS AND FEASTS

EGYPTIANS HELD FEASTS to celebrate births, marriages, and religious festivals, or just to entertain friends. The wealthy enjoyed holding dinner parties. Cooks prepared a huge meal, flavoured with imported herbs and spices. Dressed in their best clothes, guests sat on chairs or cushions on the floor, eating food with their fingers and drinking large quantities of wine.

LUTIST
Hosts hired musicians to play and sing at the feast.

Acrobat

Wine amphorae

AFTER-DINNER ENTERTAINMENT
Dinner parties were one of the main sources of employment for dancers, acrobats, and other entertainers. They performed after the meal was finished.

NEW KINGDOM BANQUET
This scene shows Egyptian hospitality at a dinner party. An army of servants ply the guests with food, wine, and presents.

Food is piled high on tables

TOO DRUNK TO WALK
Guests sometimes drank too much; some even vomited into bowls. These drunk men are being carried home from a party.

FOOD FOR THE FEAST
Pictures showing food offerings give us a good idea of the types of foods that wealthy hosts could serve their guests.

Scantily clad serving girl

Pleated clothes

Necklace presented as gift

Married couples sit arm in arm

Chair legs shaped like lions' paws

Incense cones

Servants offer wine and lotus flowers to guests

This group of women sitting together are probably unmarried

MUSIC AND DANCE

NO EGYPTIAN CELEBRATION would have been complete without music and dancing. At parties, singers performed to the music of harps, lutes, drums, flutes, and tambourines. Festival crowds chanted and clapped, carried along by the vibrant rhythm of Egyptian orchestras, while dancers leapt and twirled. Work, too, was often accompanied by music.

WOMAN PLAYING THE HARP
This model of a harpist was placed in a tomb to entertain guests at parties in the afterlife. In tomb pictures, harpists are often blind men.

SINGING ALONG
Singing played an important role in Egyptian music. These young women sing and dance, while beating tambourines and hand-held drums

Double crown of Egypt

CYMBALS
We do not know how Egyptian music sounded because it was never written down. The people played a wide range of instruments, suggesting that their music was varied. These bronze cymbals were used for rhythm and beat.

FORMATION DANCE TEAM
These men look like they are doing the cancan. Men danced with men, and women partnered women. Men and women never danced together.

Head of Horus

Tuning peg

Five strings

RATTLE
Cymbals, bells, and metal rattles, called *sistra*, were used mostly in religious music.

HARP SONG
The words that were sung to some ancient Eygptian songs have survived. "Enjoy yourself while you live" begins the Harper's Song, inscribed in the tomb of King Inyotef. First appearing in about 2300 B.C., harps could have from four to 20 strings and were sometimes as tall as a person.

CLAPPERS
Bone and ivory clappers were a bit like large castanets. Players held the clappers in one hand and banged them together.

Carved to look like hands

This harp in the shape of a pharaoh may have belonged to a court musician

Clappers were joined by twine

BUILDING AND TECHNOLOGY

SKILLS AND ARTISTRY

THE ANCIENT EGYPTIANS were very practical people. The great pyramids, tombs, and temples that still stand today show how they had mastered many architectural and engineering problems. These monuments were built and decorated by teams of skilled craftsmen, who worked year round for the pharaoh.

PLUMB LINE
Tools like this were used to make sure lines were vertical and to create grids for painting and carving on walls.

USING A MOULD
Wooden tomb models show scenes of ancient Egyptians at work. This man is busy moulding a mud brick.

MUD BRICK

Wood joints hold mould together

WOODEN BRICK MOULD

Handle

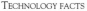

MUD BRICK AND BRICK MOULD
The Egyptians built most of their buildings with bricks. Workmen used moulds like this to shape a mixture of Nile mud, sand, and straw. Bricks were not fired, just left to dry in the hot sun.

TECHNOLOGY FACTS

• Pharaoh Khafra had 23 life-size statues of himself made for just one temple.

• The first strike in recorded history was staged by craftsmen working in the tomb of Ramses III in 1150 B.C.

• The new capital at Amarna was the first planned city in history.

BEADWORK NECKLACE

Workshops made jewellery for daily wear and for the tomb. The pharaoh sometimes ordered expensive pieces to mark special occasions or to give to foreign visitors. This funerary necklace was made c.330 B.C. The intricate beadwork incorporates tiny charms called amulets.

Faience

Coloured beads

Hawk heads represent Horus

Heh, god of longevity

Bes, a deity who warded off evil

Pectoral

Palette of pens

Stone hammer

Chisel

Three-legged stool

Ebony casket

Engraving metal vessel

Goldsmith finishing sphinx

TOMB ART

Some of the greatest art was made for the tombs of kings and nobles. On this wooden funerary stela, a priestess raises her hands in adoration of Ra-Horakhty the falcon-headed sun god.

METALWORK

There are many paintings of craft workshops. In this detail, two jewellers finish a pectoral (pendant) and place it in a casket. To the right, a man engraves an inscription, while another is working on a golden sphinx. Other scenes in the same tomb show controllers weighing gold and checking finished articles. In reality, this workshop must have been noisy, dirty, and very hot.

BOAT-BUILDING

EGYPT'S HIGHWAY was the Nile. Everything from grain and cattle to coffins and building stone was transported by water. Only the best boats were wooden, because wood was very rare. Most travellers and fishermen punted through the shallows on rafts made from bundles of reeds.

ADZE
Blade

STEERING OAR
The Egyptians steered their boats with special oars mounted on the stern (back). This brightly painted example was found in a boat pit near the pyramid of the pharaoh Senusret III (c.1850 B.C.). The Eye of Horus was a symbol of protection.

String

Bow

BOW DRILL

Drill bit

WOODWORKING TOOL
A carpenter's tools have changed little since ancient Egyptian times. Saws, chisels, and axes have all been found. This adze was used for hacking and planing, while the bow drill bored holes for pegging pieces of wood together.

Man uses adze to smooth hull

CARPENTERS AT WORK
Boat-building is an ancient craft. This tomb scene from Saqqara dates from about 2300 B.C. The Egyptians had not yet discovered iron, and all tools and pegs were made of copper and wood.

Sun canopy

Attendant

Mummy

Oars

MODEL BOAT
Egyptians put model
boats in tombs in the
belief that the boat
would carry the dead
person's mummy to
the afterlife.

Prow carved
to look like
a bundle
of papyrus

Five pairs
of oars

Priest

Royal cabin

Steersman

Steering
oars

Stern

KHUFU'S BOAT
The best preserved
boat is the funeral
barge of King Khufu.
It was found in 1954
in a sealed pit next
to his tomb, the Great
Pyramid at Giza. Made
from 651 pieces of
cedar, the boat is
43.5 m (143 ft) long.

NILE SAILBOAT

SEA-GOING SHIP

SAILING
Large sails were used to travel
upriver against the current.
Going downriver, the sail
was dropped and the boat was rowed.

CARGO BOAT

WEAPONS OF WAR

THE ARMIES of the Old and Middle Kingdoms were small, and citizens were often called up to fight. In the New Kingdom, a more professional, permanent army was established, with corps of infantry, scouts, and marines. Chariots held two soldiers; one handled the horses and the other fired arrows at the enemy.

A LONG SWORD

SHORT SWORD

DAGGER

GODDESS OF WAR
War goddess Sekhmet has a lion's head and a woman's body. She was said to stand by the pharaoh in battle, armed with arrows "with which she pierces hearts".

BLADES
Daggers with tapered copper blades were carried in wooden sheaths. Swords (first short, then long) were introduced during the New Kingdom.

FIGHTING FORMATION
Foot soldiers trained to fight in strict formation, moving together and presenting the enemy with a wall of shields. These soldiers wear kilts and carry spears.

ARROWHEADS
For thousands of years arrowheads were made from stone (especially flint), bone, or the hardwood ebony. Bronze was not used until c.1800 B.C.

FLINT HEADS

BRONZE HEADS

CHARIOTS
Introduced from the Middle East in c.1650 B.C., chariots revolutionized warfare. Here, Tutankhamun fires arrows at Nubian enemies from the raised platform of his chariot.

ARCHER
Massed units of archers led the assault. On foot or riding in chariots, they showered the enemy with arrows. Many archers came from Nubia, which Egyptians called "the Land of the Bow".

A SILVER SHAFTED AXE

CEREMONIAL AXE

AXES
Battle-axes were used all across the Middle East. The ceremonial axe was probably awarded to a warrior for bravery.

ARCHER'S AID
An archer wore this guard on the wrist of his bow hand to protect himself from the lash of the bowstring.

SOLDIER ON HORSE
The army relied on charioteers rather than on a cavalry. This rare picture is from the Greek era.

MERCENARIES
The Egyptians supplemented their own forces by relying on foreign mercenaries, who were allowed to retain their own weapons and costumes.

BATTLE AXE

THE PYRAMIDS

ALREADY ANCIENT by Tutankhamun's times, the Pyramids of Giza have awed people ever since they were built – more than 4,500 years ago. Pyramids are tombs made to house the mummies of kings. Their massive size and the precision of their construction are amazing.

▲ TRUE PYRAMID
■ BENT PYRAMID
● STEP PYRAMID

Menkaura's queens' pyramids

Menkaura's pyramid, built c.2490 B.C.

Khafra's pyramid (c.2520 B.C.)

Mortuary temple

Causeway

Valley temple

ALL THE PYRAMIDS
The biggest and best-preserved pyramids are the three at Giza. There are more than 80 others in Egypt – mostly ruins, all but buried by shifting desert sands. The first pyramids had stepped or bent sides. Then came the classic (true) shape.

THE THREE PYRAMIDS AT GIZA
From left to right, these are the pyramids of pharaohs Menkaura, Khafra, and Khufu. The three small pyramids in the foreground are "queens' pyramids". The wives and the children of King Menkaura are probably buried here.

THE SPHINX
This massive stone figure of a lion with the head of a king crouches before the pyramid complex at Giza. The Sphinx's face is believed to be a likeness of pharaoh Khafra.

PYRAMID FACTS

• The Pyramids of Giza are one of the seven wonders of the ancient world and the only one still standing.

• The four sides of the Great Pyramid are aligned exactly with true north, south, east, and west.

• A dream told Thutmose IV to free the Sphinx from the sands that buried it.

Great Pyramid, built by King Khufu c.2550 B.C.

Tombs of nobles and officials

Covered causeway linking Khufu's valley temple with mortuary temple

Cultivated land

Sphinx

River Nile

Canal linked to River Nile

GIZA COMPLEX
The dead pharaoh's mummy arrived by boat along the Nile. Mourners carried the coffin up a long causeway to the mortuary temple. Here, priests performed sacred rites before laying the dead king to rest in the prepared burial chamber, either beneath or deep inside the pyramid.

How were pyramids built?

Egyptologists estimate that it took 100,000 men 20 years to build the Great Pyramid at Giza. But how was it built? The most popular theory is that workers slid the massive blocks of stone up ramps onto the pyramid. As little real evidence exists, we will probably never know for sure.

SQUARING OFF
One tomb painting shows masons using chisels and mallets to smooth down blocks of stone.

RAMPS OR LIFTING MACHINES?

An ancient Greek traveller wrote that workers had used lifting machines to raise stones. But he was told this 2,000 years after the pyramids were built. Ramps are less work and so more likely.

Four times as many men

WERE THE PYRAMIDS BUILT LIKE THIS?

This model illustrates how the Egyptians may have built the pyramids. Workers unload the stone blocks from boats, then slide them up a long ramp to the top of the pyramid.

Mud-brick ramp is built higher as pyramid grows

Stacks of stone blocks

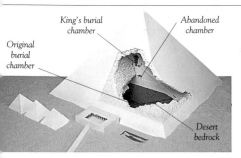

Original burial chamber

King's burial chamber

Abandoned chamber

Desert bedrock

INSIDE THE GREAT PYRAMID
A complex network of passages and dead-end chambers lies within Khufu's pyramid. Workers sealed the shaft leading to the burial chamber with huge blocks of stone.

BUILDING STONES
The pyramid core was made from local limestone. The outer layer – mostly gone now – was high-quality limestone brought by boat from Tura on the east side of the Nile, south of Giza.

Teams drag stone up on rollers

Sun shelter

Wooden scaffolding

Workers lay facing of fine Tura limestone

Entrance to underground passages and burial chamber

TEMPLES

EGYPTIAN TEMPLES were awesome structures with massive stone walls and rows of columns carved with hieroglyphs and religious images. A temple was the home of a god. Ordinary people could only enter the outer court. In dark rooms at the temple's heart, priests performed sacred rituals.

TEMPLE OF LUXOR
Ramses the Great enlarged this temple and added two obelisks and six colossal statues.

KING-SIZE SCULPTURE
Sculptors used wooden scaffolding to carve the towering statues of kings. Only the pharaoh could be shown as large as the gods in temple statues.

SON OF THE SUN GOD
The pharaoh was believed to be the son of sun god Amun. This "Birth Room" at Luxor Temple has a series of carvings that illustrate Amenhotep III's divine birth.

COLOSSI OF MEMNON
These giant figures are all that is left of the temple of Amenhotep III, the biggest ever built. A stela records that it was "inlaid with gold throughout, its floors paved with silver".

Elevated roof

Papyrus-shaped columns

Pictures of gods

90

Sanctuary, vestibules, service and music rooms

Hypostyle halls

Open court

Pylon gateway

Obelisks

Enclosure wall

Avenue of sphinxes

Sacred lake

Relief carvings of gods

Flagstaff

A TYPICAL TEMPLE COMPLEX
The temple was part of a huge complex with farms, workshops, Houses of Life (offices), and Houses of the Book (libraries). Each temple owned great tracts of land, where food was grown to be offered to the gods.

PYLON GATEWAY
People entered the temple through a pylon gateway, which was often flanked with seated statues and obelisks. High above, on wooden flagstaffs, flew the gods' flags.

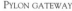

Hall contained 134 columns

HYPOSTYLE HALL AT KARNAK TEMPLE
This powerful temple owned land all over Egypt, and its priests virtually ruled the country at several periods. This is a reconstruction of Karnak's Great Hypostyle Hall. A temple symbolized the creation of the world, which is why the hall's cluster of columns were shaped like plants.

CRAFTS

IN LARGE WORKSHOPS, skilled craftsmen made pots, carved wood to make mummy cases and furniture, cured hides to produce leather, and worked metal and glass to make jewellery and everyday items such as magic amulets, tools, bowls, and even early drainpipes.

Glazed with bright pattern

STRIPED GLASS VESSEL
Glass beads were made befo[re] the pharaohs. But glass was not mass-produced until c.1400 B.C. The glass was not blown, so vessels were uneven

Wadjet eyes

Lotus flower

Birds

Antelope's head

GOLD PECTORAL
The finest jewellery was made in royal workshops. This gold pectoral – a large pendant worn on the chest – is inlaid with gemstones and coloured glass.

IVORY ANTELOPE
From predynastic times, the Egyptians used ivory from elephants and hippos to carve a variety of everyday objects. These carvings were often shaped to fit the cylindrical shape of the tusk or tooth. This skilfully crafted toilet dish was made in about 1300 B.C.

POTTERY WORKSHOP
By Old Kingdom times, pots were being made on potters' wheels. After a few days drying in the sun, pots were smoothed and then fired in kilns.

FORMING LIP OF CUP

SHAPING OUTER SURFACE

CUTTING CUP FROM CLAY BASE

STARTING A NEW CU[P]

GOLD HAWK
Metals were smelted over an open
fire. Before the New Kingdom, when
bellows were invented, rows of men
stoked the fire by blowing down pipes.
The liquid metal was poured into a mould, cooled, and beaten
into shape. Dipping in liquid gold was one way to gild objects.

Feather detail

Hollow for mummy

CAT MUMMY CASE
Carpenters made items for both homes
and tombs. Because of the shortage
of wood, these craftsmen excelled
at joining small pieces together
by dovetailing. The two halves
of this mummy case fit snugly
together thanks
to wooden
dowels.

Dented and worn

WOODEN MALLET

TOOLS OF THE TRADE
A carpenter's main tools
were wooden mallets,
flint scrapers, and bronze-
bladed axes, saws, adzes,
chisels, and bow drills.

Nut top

PIERCERS
Animal
hides were
cured with the
mineral alum. Then
saddlers used piercers
and knives to make leather
sandals, ropes, and bags.

PATTING DUNG

STOKING DUNG-
BURNING KILN

CUPS ARE
PLACED IN KILN

FIRED CUPS ARE
CARRIED AWAY

EGYPTIAN ART

THE BEAUTIFUL ART of ancient Egypt was produced by teams of anonymous painters and sculptors. They worked in tombs, temples, palaces, and houses. Their art is highly stylized; figures are almost always depicted in formal poses, and it is difficult to recognize individuals because most subjects are given perfect features.

aArtists used grids to calculate "divine proportions"

AGRIDLINES

Artists began by drawing a grid. Then they sketched in figures and objects, scaled up from examples in pattern books. Master designers checked and made corrections before work began.

PERIOD STYLES

Each period had its own distinctive artistic style. The art of the Amarna period is dramatically different. This statue of King Akhenaten has the heavy hips and long, oddly distorted face that are typical of the time.

IN A PAINTER'S WORKSHOP

Painters worked on wooden panels or straight onto statues or walls. They applied the paint in flat blocks of colour, with no shading or gradations of tone.

SOME CHARACTERISTICS OF EGYPTIAN ART

Artists portrayed everything in its most recognizable form. For example, the human body was shown in profile, but the eyes and chest were face forwards. Hieroglyphs were like a caption to the picture.

SKETCHING

Artists worked out ideas with scale models or rough sketches on ostraca (fragments of stone or broken pottery).

ART FACTS

• Tools and paints were so precious that foremen issued them each morning and locked them away at night.

• Fragments of a gigantic statue were found at Tanis. The big toe is the size of a man.

MUMMY CASE

The imagery of religious art had deep meaning to the Egyptians. The gods and symbols painted on mummy cases and tombs were to help the dead avoid the dangers of the underworld.

95

Sculpture and carvings

Ancient Egypt was rich in stone, and sculpture was the most important artform. Copper or bronze tools were used to carve softer materials like limestone and fine woods. These could then be coated with a plaster mixture called *gesso* and painted in bright colours. Hard stone, such as granite, was carved with pounders made of stone.
Metal was cast or else beaten into shape.

RAISED RELIEF
This is an example of raised relief, in which the background is cut away to leave the figures raised above the surface.

Ready for crown

SUNK RELIEF
In sunk relief, the outlines of the figures are first gouged out. Then the details within each figure are modelled at various depths. This is a sunk relief of Pharaoh Thutmose III (*c.*1450 B.C.).

Drawn guidelines

THE FACE OF QUEEN NEFERTITI
Unfinished statues give us many clues about the way sculptors worked. This half-finished bust, marked with guidelines, was found in the ruins of a workshop in the abandoned city of Amarna

TWO HEADS OF KING USERKAF

Each stone has its own qualities, making it suitable for certain purposes. Here are two heads of the same king. The colossal one is carved in granite, the smaller one in schist.

Pink speckled Aswan granite

LOST WAX METHOD

This bronze figure of King Thutmose IV was made by the lost wax method. The figure was modelled in beeswax. This was then coated in clay and heated until the wax melted. Finally, liquid metal was poured into the clay mould.

Eyes are set in copper

LOOKING LIFE-LIKE

Some statues have inset eyes. This man's eyes are made from calcite with brown obsidian irises. The effect is so life-like that the eyes seem to follow you around a room. This is the head of the seated scribe, shown on page 22.

GRANITE PHARAOH

Kings' statues were usually carved from hard stone, as they were made to last. This 3,500-year-old granite statue of King Sobkemsaf proves that they did.

RELIGION

WORSHIP AND BELIEFS

LIKE OTHER ANCIENT PEOPLE, Egyptians believed that all events were controlled by the gods. By wearing amulets (lucky charms) and giving offerings to the gods, the Egyptians hoped for a happy life. They also hoped the gods would help them to live on after death.

ANIMAL GODS
Many gods were thought to live on earth inside animals. This ram-headed sphinx represents the god Amun.

PROTECTED BY THE GODS
This mummy case is covered in images of gods and magic symbols meant to help the dead person in the afterlife. A Greek wrote that Egyptians were "religious beyond measure, more than any other nation".

Spell for the soul of the dead person

Tomb

Mummy is made ready for the tomb

REPRESENTING THE PHARAOH
The gods were kept happy by priests, who made offerings and conducted rituals in the name of the pharaoh, the sun god's representative on earth. Here, priests perform rights to help the dead person achieve eternal life.

THREE MUMMIFIED HEADS

To live forever, Egyptians had to have their bodies, especially their faces, preserved in a lifelike way. This way the spirit of a dead person could recognize its body when it returned to the tomb.

Carrying pole

Servant with fan

CARRIED AWAY

A rich man was buried with this model of a sedan chair carried by three porters. He expected them to come to life after his tomb was sealed.

FACTS ABOUT RELIGION

• The sacred Apis Bull was treated like a god, kept in a luxurious part of the temple, fed the best food, and buried like a pharaoh when it died.

• Many Egyptians were buried with 365 *shabti* figures – one to help on each day of the year.

VIEW OF HEAVEN

In the ideal world shown on his funerary stela, Iy smells flowers with his family. The stela would keep his name alive as he lived these scenes in the afterlife.

MYTHS AND LEGENDS

THE EGYPTIAN CREATION STORY has many
versions – most begin in an ocean of
chaos. There were hundreds of other
myths and legends. But because
everyone knew the stories, they
were never written down, and few
have survived. Luckily, the
story of god-king Osiris and
his victory over death was
recorded by a Greek writer.

IN THE BEGINNING
One creation myth tells of a time
when Nun, the eternal ocean,
filled the universe. When the
waters subsided a primeval hill
appeared, on which stood the
creator god – the sun god Atum.

ATUM

*Isis nurses
the infant
Horus, her
son by Osiris*

THE GODS ARE CREATED
Atum's children, Shu (air) and Tefnut (moisture) created Geb
(earth) and Nut (sky). At first Geb and Nut were joined, but
Shu came between them – so separating heaven and earth. Geb
and Nut had four children – Osiris, Seth, Isis, and Nephthys.

ISIS AND HORUS
Osiris became king
and took sister Isis
as his queen. Jealous
brother Seth killed
Osiris and cut up the
body. Isis collected
the pieces and made
them into the first
mummy. Osiris
lived on as god of
the underworld.

Corn, not a body, fills the bandages

Wadjet Eye amulets were placed on mummies

WADJET EYE

When he grew up, Horus set out to avenge his father's death. Eventually, he vanquished Seth and took the throne. But in their many fights he lost an eye. This Eye of Horus, or *Wadjet* Eye, became a symbol of victory over evil.

MURDER OF A BROTHER

Seth held a banquet where he showed off a beautiful casket, saying he would give it to whoever fitted inside. When Osiris climbed in, Seth locked it and threw it in the Nile. Isis found the casket, but Seth seized it and cut up Osiris' body.

OSIRIS

This is a corn mummy in the shape of Osiris. At first he was a fertility god, responsible for the floods that brought new life to Egypt every year. As the first king to survive death, he became a god of rebirth.

SACRED SHAPES

According to legend, the rays of the sun fell first of all upon the primeval mound, or *ben-ben*. This sacred shape was recreated in obelisks and may have been the reason for the structure of pyramids.

SUN TEMPLE

THE SUN GODS

SOURCE OF ALL HEAT AND LIGHT, the sun
was worshipped from earliest times. This life-
giving force took many forms, each represente
by a different god or personality. The rising
sun was a scarab beetle; at noon it was Ra, th
orange disc itself; while in the evening it took
the form of a ram. Satirical literary texts depic
the setting sun as a dribbling, decrepit old man

AMUN-RA
During the New
Kingdom, power
moved to Thebes in
the south. Theban
priests merged their
local god Amun, a
creator god, with the
powerful sun god Ra.
Throughout the land,
Egyptians worshipped
Amun-Ra as chief god.

*Akhenaten and his
family worship Aten*

AKHENATEN, THE SUN KING
To break the power of the Theban
priesthood, King Amenhotep IV
banned all gods but Aten, the sun
in its purest form. It was depicted as
a disc with rays that touched with
human hands. The king changed his
name to Akhenaten and built a new
city dedicated to Aten at Amarna.

WINGED SCARAB

The scarab is a beetle that rolls up balls of dung to lay its eggs inside. Egyptians believed that a giant scarab made the sun in the same way and then rolled it over the horizon and across the sky.

Scarab god clasps the sun in its claws

Prayers to the sun god

SAILING THROUGH THE NIGHT

When the sun set in the West, the Egyptians believed it sailed through the underworld on a boat before rising again in the East. Here, the god Nun steers the boat safely through the waters of chaos.

IMHOTEP

The cult of the sun began at Heliopolis. Here, King Djoser's chief minister Imhotep designed the first pyramid – possibly as a stairway, so the dead pharaoh could join the sun god in the sky.

SUN STRUCK

Heliopolis means "Sun City". In its temple, priests kept a triangular stone, the *ben-ben* – believed to be the first object struck by the sun's rays when the world was created. This tomb cap is carved in the same magical shape.

RA-HARAKHTY

Sun gods are usually depicted with the disc of the sun on their heads. The god on the far right is Ra-Harakhty, a falcon-headed sun god and a version of the sky god Horus.

GODS AND GODDESSES

EGYPTIANS HAD A DIZZYING number of gods – one ancient text lists 740. But only a small number were worshipped in the same place at the same time. All the forces of nature were represented by gods or goddesses. Temples were dedicated to state gods or important local deities and controlled by an elite priesthood. Ordinary people were excluded.

Ptah is depicted with a tight skull cap pulled over his shaven head

Flail

PTAH
The cult centre of this god was Memphis, capital city during the Old Kingdom. By New Kingdom times Ptah had become a state god. He is always shown as a man, wrapped up like a mummy. He was a creator god and a patron of craftsmen.

WOLF GOD WEPWAWET
This god from Lycopolis in Middle Egypt was associated with war and life after death. On this stela, the dead man bows before Wepwawet in the hope that the god will help him to live forever.

MIN
The fertility god Min wears two tall plumes on his hat and holds a flail – an agricultural tool. One of his symbols was lettuce, which the Egyptians considered a fertility food.

MAAT

The basic laws of the universe – justice, truth, and order – were represented by the goddess Maat. Her name meant "straight". She wore the *feather of Truth* on her head. Maat is often shown as a doll, held by the sun god Ra.

Palette and pen

THOTH

Many gods were associated with animals. For example, Thoth, the god of writing and wisdom, was depicted as an ibis – a bird that the Egyptians thought was wise. Here he is shown as an ibis-headed man writing with a scribe's pen and palette.

HATHOR

Some gods had different roles in different parts of Egypt. Hathor, goddess of love, music, and dance, was shown as a woman or a cow. In the Delta she was associated with the sky and held the sun between her horns. In Thebes she was a goddess of death.

KHNUM

This ram-headed creator god is sometimes shown moulding people on a potter's wheel. At Aswan, Khnum was guardian of the Nile and worshipped as "he who brought the flood".

BASTET

Worship of the cat goddess Bastet began at Bubastis, in the Delta. In later times she became popular all over Egypt, and her annual festival was a national celebration.

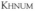

MAGIC AND POPULAR RELIGION

THE STATE GODS played little part in normal life. If they had a sick child or a son at war, Egyptians asked protection from more down-to-earth gods. People wore amulets (lucky charms) and recited prayers and spells to ward off disease or disaster.

BES
Part dwarf and part lion, Bes was a popula household god. He carried a knife and a musical instrument whose sweet sounds warded off bad spirit

Taweret was shown as a pregnant hippo

OFFERING SHRINE
Like most ancient people, the Egyptians tried to please the gods by giving offerings of food and drink. They did this at temples, in chapels set up next to tombs, or in small shrines inside the home.

Lotus-bud shape

TAWERET
Childbirth was dangerous, both for the mother and the baby. Egyptians prayed and put their faith in Taweret, the goddess of childbirth.

MAGIC WAN
This magical stick wa made from a hippo tusk. It carved with powerful symbols, and could be used to create a defensive barri around a part of the house. These wands we also used to protect a child or a sick perso

HOUSE CHARM

This stela asks god Horus to protect the family from the dangers of daily life. He tramples on two crocodiles and grips snakes, lions, and scorpions in his hands. Above Horus' head, Bes pokes his tongue out at evil spirits. Magic spells cover the stela's sides.

MEDICAL TOOLS

Egyptians believed in magic, but they were also highly skilled at medicine. This temple carving shows a range of medical instruments, including forceps. One papyrus lists over 700 prescriptions for different ailments, grouped according to the sick organ.

Mythological creature

Broken amulet

Thoth as a baboon

PROTECTIVE NECKLACE

People wore amulets in their jewellery. This necklace has the goddess Taweret, the gods Horus and Thoth, and a lion to defend the wearer from any harm. Similar amulets were tucked in the wrappings of mummies.

Frog represented the goddess Hekat, who protected women in childbirth

Hawk-headed Horus

Taweret

A lion for defence

PRIESTS AND RITUALS

ANCIENT EGYPTIAN PRIESTS were called "servants of the gods". Their job was not to preach to the people, but to keep the gods happy and fulfilled. They did this by performing elaborate rituals in the sacred inner sanctums of temples, where only senior priests and the pharaoh were allowed to enter.

Cup for burning incense

PURE ONE
To show their purity, priests shaved their heads and bodies and washed many times a day. This man burns incense and sprinkles water from the sacred lake. In the inner sanctum of the temple, the priest chanted "I am a Pure One" as he approached the gold statue of the god.

Hair in sidelock of youth

Offering table

Bucket held water from sacred lake

CHILD PRIEST
There were many different classes of priests. This one wears his hair in a sidelock of youth, not because of his age, but to show that he is acting as the loving son of the god.

SITULA (SACRED BUCKET)

INCENSE BURNER
As incense burns, it lets off a mild, sweet-smelling smoke. It was used to purify temples and to please the gods that lived in them. The handle of this incense burner is shaped like the sky god Horus.

Holder for incense

Sacred tool

Hawk head

Leopard skin

RITUAL TOOL
Here, King Ay holds a sacred tool to perform the *Opening of the Mouth* ceremony on the mummy of Tutankhamun. He wears the leopard-skin robe of a priest.

Eye of Horus

51067

Priest worships goddess Mut

Leg of meat

MIRROR
At the heart of the temple was a gold statue of the god. The priests washed it, dressed it, and placed food before it several times a day. The god was sealed in its shrine at night, then "woken" in the morning. This is a god's vanity mirror.

Head of moon god Khons

Ivory handle

FOOD OFFERINGS
This offering tray is inscribed with pictures of food. The food that the priests offered to the god was grown on the temple's large estates. In reality, the god did not touch the food – the priests ate it later on.

DEATH AND BURIAL

THE EGYPTIANS WANTED TO LIVE forever. To achieve this, they believed that a dead person's body had to be preserved, or "mummified". The mummy was then buried with elaborate rites and a book of magic spells to help it in its journey through the treacherous underworld.

Pieces of gold leaf

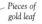

GIRL MUMMY
This is the body of a girl who died over 2,000 years ago, aged eight or nine. Her body was coated in oils and resins to stop it from decaying and then covered in gold leaf – maybe because Ra, the sun god, was believed to have a skin of gold.

Ba *bird*   Mummy

THE MUMMY'S SOUL
Egyptians believed that a person's spirit took several forms. One of these was the Ba, similar to a soul. The *Ba* – depicted as a bird – left the body at death. Only when it returned would the person live forever.

TOMB OWNERS

Statues of the dead were placed in the tomb chapel to make sure that the gods knew who was buried there. Loved ones visited the chapel to put offerings before the statues.

Husband and wife

ANUBIS

The god of death and embalming was the jackal-headed Anubis. He was thought to guard mummies and necropolises (burial grounds). A priest wearing an Anubis mask supervised the ritual practices that surrounded the process of embalming (preserving).

A HUMBLE HEAVEN

The Egyptians' idea of heaven was a rural paradise, presided over by the god Osiris. They called it the *Field of Reeds* – a place where the sun shone and people worked in the fields, planting and harvesting their crops. In fact, it was just like Egypt – except grain grew a foot taller.

Head of a jackal

The dead were often shown in the doorway

Body of a man

FALSE DOOR

Tomb walls contained false doors – gateways between the worlds of the living and the dead. The spirits of the dead were thought to come and go through these doorways.

FUNERAL PROCESSION

Mourners wailed and splashed their faces with mud, as priests dragged the mummy to the tomb. Before sealing the mummy in, the priests performed sacred rites and repeated magic spells.

PROTECTIVE EYE
Cuts made in the
flesh were covered with
plates like this one. It
bears a sacred symbol,
the Eye of Horus, to
protect the body.

PREPARING A MUMMY

TO STOP IT FROM ROTTING away, a body
was preserved by embalming. After the
internal organs were removed, the
corpse was washed, dried out with
natural salts, and then coated with
oils and resins. Finally, it was wrapped
in many layers of tight linen bandages.
The whole process took 70 days.

Natron

RITUAL KNIVES
The internal organs were removed
through an incision cut in the
abdomen. The brain was drawn out
with a hook passed through the nose.

Duamutef guarded the stomach

CANOPIC JARS
Intestines, lungs,
stomach, and liver
were mummified
separately and put
in four canopic jars.
The lids depicted
gods, who stopped
evil forces using
the organs in spells
against the dead.

PRESERVING SALT
To stop decay, a body must be
thoroughly dried out. The Egyptians
did this with dry crystals of natron,
a natural salt found by desert lakes.
The procedure took 40 days.

KEEPING HER HAIR

This skull of a woman is 3,500 years old. Skin and flesh have rotted away, leaving nothing but hair and bone. Every hair was saved and then placed in the tomb, because a lost strand could be used in spells against her.

Teeth can give clues about age and diet

Plaited hair

Linen bandages

MUMMY OF A BOY

A mummy could be wrapped in more than 20 layers of bandages. As each one was added, it was brushed with oils and resins.

OPENING THE MOUTH

During mummification there were constant prayers and rituals. The most important was the *Opening of the Mouth*, held just before burial. It was meant to restore the mummy's senses.

WRAPPED UP

Before wrapping, the dried body was stuffed with linen and sawdust to restore shape. Sunken cheeks might be padded out and artificial eyes put in.

MUMMY LABEL

Embalming was done by special priests. They made sure body parts were not mixed up by tying labels to the mummies.

JOURNEY TO THE AFTERLIFE

TO REACH HEAVEN, the Egyptians believed that a dead person had to travel through *Duat*, the underworld, where monsters and lakes of fire awaited. To fight them, the mummy was forearmed with a collection of magic spells, written in the *Book of the Dead*. The book included a map of *Duat* and many prayers to ward off evil.

BOX OF WORKERS
Shabtis are model workers placed in the tomb. They are inscribed with Chapter Six of the *Book of the Dead*

Anubis takes dead man to be judged · Scales · Jury of gods · Monster Ammit

STILL TALKING
This tomb model of a man and wife chatting shows how Egyptians expected life to be much the same after death. They crammed their tombs with jewellery, clothes, food, games, make-up, and anything else they might need in the afterlife.

EXTRA PROTECTION
Amulets – magic charms worn like jewellery or put into the wrappings – also helped protect a mummy from evil. The *djed* pillar was thought to give strength.

Ptah-Sokar-Osiris wearing Atef *crown and false beard*

*a*Base of statue

Scroll

Secret compartment

DJED PILLAR

ROLLED UP
The Book of the Dead
was written on scrolls of papyrus and put in the tomb. This statue of composite god Ptah-Sokar-Osiris has a hidden compartment where the scroll was kept.

Osiris, god of the nderworld, presides over judgement

Goddess Nephthys with sister Isis

WEIGHING THE HEART
The final test came in the *Hall of the Two Truths*. Here, Anubis weighed the dead person's heart to see if it was heavy with sin. If it was lighter than the *Feather of Truth*, the person lived forever. If not, the heart was thrown to the monster Ammit, "Devourer of the Dead".

HEART PROTECTOR
Pectorals are amulets that were laid on the mummy's chest to guard the heart, a symbol of life. Many were inscribed with pleas like "See, this heart of mine, it weeps and pleads for mercy".

MUMMY CASES

THE FINISHED MUMMY was laid in a coffin, or mummy case. Like the tomb, this case was seen as a "house" for the dead person's spirit. Mummy cases changed gradually through the course of history, but from the earliest days the Egyptians covered them with magic symbols and pleas to the gods.

WOODEN CASE
For a long time all mummy cases were wooden. In later times many inner cases were made of cheaper cartonnage – layers of papyrus or linen, pressed together like papier mâché.

Mummy was sealed inside while cartonnage was still wet

LACED IN TIGHT
Many mummies were buried in two or three cases – one inside the other like Russian dolls. The tight-fitting inner case was laced up at the back.

Reed matting tied with twine ropes

MASKED MUMMY
This mummy of a woman is wearing a painted mask over her head and shoulders. She is also decked out in a wide selection of protective amulets.

BABY COFFIN
The earliest coffins, from about 3000 B.C., were simple reed baskets. This later example (c.1400 B.C.) contains the body of a baby. Bone deformities indicate death due to serious illness.

LOOKING GOOD
The mummy case usually presented an idealized portrait of the dead person. Analysis of this youthful-looking mummy shows that he was about 50 when he died.

FACTORY FACE
This is a wooden portrait from a coffin. Sometimes the face was made separately and pegged onto the case. These carved features were often mass produced. Regional styles allow experts to identify the area of Egypt.

SAFELY INSIDE
The priests in charge of embalming secure a mummy in its case. Wooden cases were held together with thick pegs.

WOODEN BOX
A pharaoh or an important official had an extra stone coffin, or sarcophagus. These massive structures were extremely heavy and difficult to move. This priest (Hor) had an extra wooden box instead.

Painted gods

Spells in hieroglyphs

Animal mummies

Beetles, birds, cats, crocodiles – the
Egyptians mummified an amazing array of creatures.
Some were beloved household pets. But most animals
were mummified because of their association with
particular gods. In later times, millions of animals
were bred just to be mummified and buried in special
cemeteries dedicated to the gods. Four million ibis
mummies were found in one cemetery, each in its own pot.

Painted face

Geometric wrappings, a feature of the Roman period

CAT MUMMY
Egyptians were the first
people to keep cats
as pets. The earliest
written mention dates
from 2100 B.C. They
probably tamed
African wild cats, a
species that was the
ancestor of all modern
pets. Cats were linked
with goddess Bastet.

Carved falcon, symbol of the sky god Horus

Anubis, god of embalming

IBIS
This large
wading bird
is still common
in the marshes
by the Nile. It
was sacred to
Thoth, the
god of writing
and wisdom and
patron of scribes.
Biologists have used
mummies and ancient
pictures of ibises to show
that the species has not
changed in 5,000 years.

FOUR FALCONS
The falcon was king
of the Egyptian skies
and was seen as a
representative of
the sky god Horus.
This case contains
four falcon mummies
and is painted with
funerary scenes.

UNWRAPPED CROCODILE
Crocodiles were sacred to the water god Sobek. Priests kept pet crocodiles in luxury, feeding them on the best meat and wines.

Ears are flattened against skull

Fur

UNDER THE LINEN
The legs of this unwrapped cat mummy have been tucked in to make a compact shape. Many of these cats were bred by priests just to be mummified and sold to worshippers visiting the temples.

PRESERVED FISH
Other animals found as mummies include fish, vultures, owls, baboons, rats, snakes, mice, dogs, geese, scarab beetles, shrews, lizards, rams, and huge bulls.

Tail curled up between legs

Case has door at back

Each case contained a cat mummy

CAT CASES
These cat mummy cases all come from Bubastis, sacred city of Bastet. In later times, the festival of Bastet was an important yearly event. Huge celebrations were held in honour of the goddess, and hunting lions was forbidden.

VALLEY OF THE KINGS

DURING THE NEW KINGDOM, the capital city moved to Thebes in the south, and pharaohs were buried in the desolate Valley of the Kings. These royal tombs were hidden, cut deep into the rock. Steep steps and cramped passages led to the burial chamber, where the pharaoh's mummy lay surrounded by fabulous treasures.

VALLEY VIEW
The ancient Egyptians called the Valley of the Kings *The Great Place*. Neighbouring Valley of the Queens was known as *The Place of Beauty*. This view across the Nile shows the temple of Queen Hatshepsut.

OVERSEER
The workers who built the kings' tombs lived in the nearby village of Deir el-Medina. A few, like the overseer Sennedjem, had beautifully painted tombs.

STAR-STUDDED CEILING
The Egyptians decorated tomb walls with exquisite paintings and reliefs. This is their view of the northern sky at night, from Sety I's tomb. Animals represent constellations, which are named in heiroglyphs.

Red spots represent bright stars

Egyptians could tell the time from the position of constellations

TOMB OF RAMSES IX
This pharaoh tried accused tomb robbers.
One confessed "We took gold and jewels
and the precious metal of his coffins. Then
we found the queen and took everything
that was hers and set fire to the coffins".

VALLEY TODAY
In ancient times, the valley was guarded.
In spite of this, thieves had looted almost
every tomb by 1000 B.C. Today, tombs in
the valley are threatened by ground water,
pollution, and endless crowds of tourists.

MAN AT WORK
This sketch shows
a bald, unshaven
mason using a
chisel and mallet.
Building the tombs
was hot, thirsty work.

The Egyptians called this
constellation Mes

Crocodile rides
on hippo's back

The sun
disc

Tutankhamun's tomb

In 1922, the English archaeologist Howard Carter found the tomb of a little known pharaoh, buried 3,200 years earlier in the Valley of the Kings. Crammed inside were priceless treasures that amazed the world. As Carter said, "There were rooms full of gold, everywhere the glint of gold".

Crook and flail, symbols of the pharaoh's power

Squatting baboon gods

INNER COFFIN
The dead pharaoh was buried in three mummy cases, one inside another. The outer two shine with gold leaf, but the inner case is made from solid gold and inlaid with gemstones. This coffin weighs an incredible 110 kg (245 lb).

BURIAL CHAMBER
The outer coffin has now been returned to the stone sarcophagus in Tutankhamun's burial chamber. The walls are painted with gods and scenes from the underworld.

SHRINE DETAIL
The sarcophagus was housed in four wooden shrines, fitting one inside another. All four glittered with gold-leaf decoration.

MUMMY MASK

The most famous treasure is the portrait mask, which covered the pharaoh's head as he lay in state. He wears a falcon-headed collar, false beard, and striped *nemes* headdress. Made from solid gold inlaid with gemstones, this masterpiece weighs 10.2 kg (22.5 lb).

PAINSTAKING WORKER

Carter catalogued every detail of his work. It took him ten seasons to clear the tomb. By the time of his death, in 1939, he had published three volumes of notes.

PILED HIGH

Here, the throne can be seen as it was found. The tomb's four rooms were piled high with treasures. It had been prepared in a hurry, probably because the king died suddenly. Later the entrance was blocked by accident, so the tomb was forgotten for more than 3,000 years.

MUMMY

The king's mummy was inside his inner coffin. In separate miniature coffins were two tiny mummies, probably his stillborn twin daughters.

THE GOLDEN THRONE

This is made of carved wood inlaid with intricate designs. The back panel shows the king and his wife.

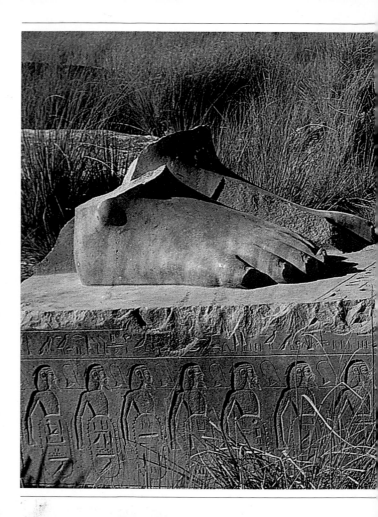

THE END OF
AN ERA

FOREIGN PHARAOHS

THE SPLENDOURS of the New Kingdom ended with the death of Ramses XI in 1069 B.C. The empire was gone, and Egypt was once again split by war and chaos. In the centuries that followed, the country was invaded by its powerful neighbours. Egyptian culture still thrived, but life by the Nile was not as stable.

POWERFUL PRIESTS
The priests of Amun at Karnak Temple near Thebes became so powerful that they were able to challenge the authority of the pharaoh. This helped lead to the collapse of the New Kingdom.

TEMPLE OF AMUN
AT KARNAK

CAPTIVE ENEMY
Egypt's traditional enemies came from what is now the Middle East. They included Babylonians, Hyksos, Hittites, and the Persians, who ruled Egypt twice (525-359 and 343-332 B.C.).

LIBYAN MUMMY
This is the mummy case of a Libyan called Pasenhor. Many Libyans settled in the Delta, and their chiefs ruled Egypt from 945 to 715 B.C. The Libyan pharaohs were resident kings, who wrote in Egyptian scripts and worshipped Egyptian gods.

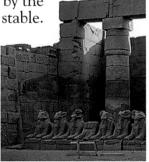

CAT WORSHIP

The Libyan kings moved their northern capital from Tanis to Bubastis, city of cat goddess Bastet. She became one of the most popular Egyptian gods and was worshipped all over Egypt.

STRONG NEIGHBOURS

For many centuries, Egypt was the only great power. But its neighbours developed and, one by one, they overran its borders. Libyan and Nubian kings lived like native Egyptians, but Assyria and Persia ruled Egypt as a colony.

ASSYRIA
SYRIA
PERSIA
LIBYA • Memphis
EGYPT • Thebes
ARABIA
NUBIA

NUBIAN KING

This is Taharqo, one of the Nubian kings. They ruled Egypt from 747 to 656 B.C. Their empire was bigger than Egypt at its height.

Egyptian gods

FACTS ABOUT THE ERA

• The Nubian pharaohs were buried in pyramids in the desert of Sudan.

• The Persians introduced the camel.

• According to legend, Alexander the Great was mummified and laid in a glass coffin floating in honey. It has never been found.

THE GREEKS

ALEXANDER THE GREAT conquered Egypt in 332 B.C.
He built a new capital city, Alexandria, on the coast.
When he died, his general Ptolemy founded a dynasty
that ruled Egypt for 300 years. The new rulers spoke
Greek and followed Greek law. But they respected the
local culture, which
continued to flourish.

TEMPLE OF ISIS AT PHILAE
The Greeks built many great temples
in Egypt, dedicated to the Egyptian
gods. On the walls, the Ptolemies
were shown as pharaohs. But these
Greek rulers rarely left Alexandria on
the Mediterranean coast, and there
were regular revolts against them.

ALEXANDER THE GREAT (356-323 B.C)
This great war leader was born in
Macedonia, part of the Greek empire.
Shortly after he became king, at age
20, he conquered the entire Persian
empire, including Egypt, Syria, and
Mesopotamia. His huge empire broke
up after he died suddenly of a fever.

FOUR DIFFERENT SCRIPTS

Greek became the official language under the Ptolemies. Hieroglyphs were only used for religious inscriptions; priests wrote in demotic. Many documents were still written in hieratic. This detail from the Rosetta Stone shows the same text in Greek and demotic.

GREEK MUMMY MASK

The invaders adopted many local traditions. The mix of Greek and Egyptian art and religion created many new hybrids. This mummy mask has realistic Greek-style features and the headdress of a wealthy Egyptian.

CLEOPATRA FROM TEMPLE OF HATHOR, DENDERA

Lotus flowers

Body of lion

Greek-style sculpture of an Egyptian icon

ALEXANDRIA

This city became an important cultural centre, famous for its lighthouse and library. The library – the greatest in the Classical World – burnt down. This sphinx was part of the library complex.

CLEOPATRA VII (69-30 B.C.)

The last Ptolemaic ruler was Cleopatra VII. She tried to save Egypt from the Romans, using her legendary charm to seduce first Julius Caesar and then Mark Anthony. But, when Roman general Octavian invaded Egypt in 30 B.C., she killed herself.

THE ROMANS

EGYPT BECAME A ROMAN state after
the conquest by Octavian in 30 B.C.
The Roman capital was Alexandria,
but the emperors ruled from Rome and
took little interest in local traditions.
Not surprisingly, there were regular
uprisings. In A.D. 642,
Egypt was invaded
by Muslim armies.

AUGUSTUS (63 B.C.-A.D. 14)
Octavian, Egypt's conqueror,
became Emperor Augustus
Caesar. He made Egypt the
granary of Rome, forcing
the country to export huge
quantities of wheat to feed
the rest of the Roman empire.

Real rings

MUMMY CASE
Mummification of
the dead continued
under the Romans.
Some mummy cases
show the dead person
dressed in their best
clothes. This Roman
woman is wearing a
colourful toga, sandals,
and wig. Her jewellery
even includes real
gold rings.

PORTRAIT
During Roman times,
a portrait, painted on
a wooden panel, was
often put over the face
of the dead person and
secured by bandages.
Painted from life, this
portrait may have
hung in the house
until the sitter died.

GOLD PARTS

Shaped pieces of gold leaf were placed over tongues, eyes, and other body parts of Roman mummies in the belief that these would restore the various functions in the afterlife.

Bunch of flowers

Gold tongue to allow mummy to speak

MUMMY MASK

This Roman mummy mask is probably one of many made in a factory from an original model. Typical of the period, he is holding a candle and a bunch of flowers, which are both symbols of rebirth.

HADRIAN (A.D. 76-138)

The only emperor to take much interest in Egypt, Hadrian was fascinated by its culture. He brought these statues back to grace his villa near Rome. He also founded a new city, named Antinoopolis, at the spot by the Nile where his lover drowned.

This area of the villa was inspired by Canopus, an Egyptian town

Pair of ducks   *Crocodile*   *Songbird on water plant*   *Ibis*

NILE SCENE

Alexandria was a centre of art. Workshops there produced many frescoes and mosaics, which were exported all over the Roman empire. This Nile-scene mosaic comes from a villa in Pompeii, Italy.

REFERENCE SECTION

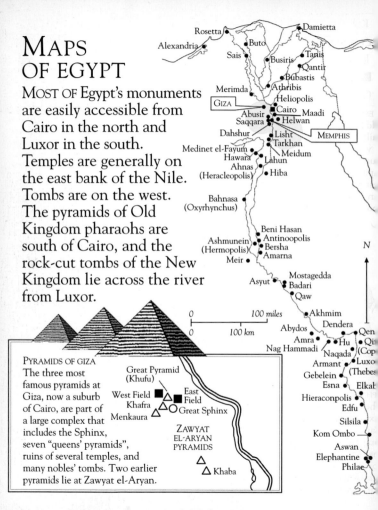

MAPS OF EGYPT

MOST OF Egypt's monuments are easily accessible from Cairo in the north and Luxor in the south. Temples are generally on the east bank of the Nile. Tombs are on the west. The pyramids of Old Kingdom pharaohs are south of Cairo, and the rock-cut tombs of the New Kingdom lie across the river from Luxor.

Rosetta

Damietta

Alexandria

Buto

Sais

Tanis

Busiris

Qantir

Bubastis

Merimda

Athribis

GIZA

Heliopolis

Cairo Maadi

Abusir

Saqqara Helwan

Dahshur

Lisht

MEMPHIS

Medinet el-Fayum

Tarkhan

Hawara

Meidum

Ahnas

Lahun

(Heracleopolis)

Hiba

Bahnasa

(Oxyrhynchus)

Beni Hasan

Antinoopolis

Ashmunein

Bersha

(Hermopolis)

Amarna

Meir

Mostagedda

Asyut

Badari

Qaw

Akhmim

Abydos

Dendera

Amra

Hu

Qen

Nag Hammadi

Naqada

Qi

Armant

(Cop

Gebelein

(Thebes)

Luxo

Esna

Elkab

Hieraconpolis

Edfu

Silsila

Kom Ombo

Aswan

Elephantine

Philae

N

0   100 miles

0   100 km

PYRAMIDS OF GIZA
The three most famous pyramids at Giza, now a suburb of Cairo, are part of a large complex that includes the Sphinx, seven "queens' pyramids", ruins of several temples, and many nobles' tombs. Two earlier pyramids lie at Zawyat el-Aryan.

Great Pyramid
(Khufu)

West Field

East Field

Khafra

Great Sphinx

Menkaura

ZAWYAT
EL-ARYAN
PYRAMIDS

Khaba

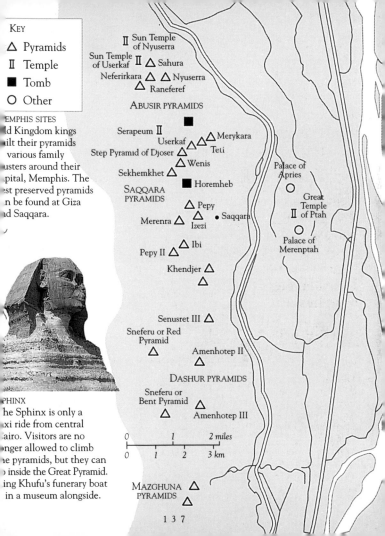

KEY

△ Pyramids
Ⅱ Temple
■ Tomb
○ Other

MEMPHIS SITES

[Ol]d Kingdom kings [bu]ilt their pyramids [in] various family [cl]usters around their [ca]pital, Memphis. The [be]st preserved pyramids [ca]n be found at Giza [an]d Saqqara.

Ⅱ Sun Temple of Nyuserra

Sun Temple of Userkaf Ⅱ △ Sahura

Neferirkara △ △ Nyuserra

△ Raneferef

ABUSIR PYRAMIDS

■

Serapeum Ⅱ

Userkaf △ △ △ Merykara

Step Pyramid of Djoser △ Teti

△ Wenis

Sekhemkhet △

■ Horemheb

SAQQARA PYRAMIDS

△ Pepy

Merenra △ △ • Saqqara

Izezi

Pepy II △ △ Ibi

Khendjer △

Senusret III △

Sneferu or Red Pyramid

△

Amenhotep II △

DASHUR PYRAMIDS

Sneferu or Bent Pyramid △

△ Amenhotep III

Palace of Apries

○

Ⅱ Great Temple of Ptah

Palace of Merenptah

0 ___ 1 ___ 2 miles

0 _ 1 _ 2 _ 3 km

MAZGHUNA △ PYRAMIDS △

SPHINX

[T]he Sphinx is only a [ta]xi ride from central [C]airo. Visitors are no [lo]nger allowed to climb [th]e pyramids, but they can [go] inside the Great Pyramid. [K]ing Khufu's funerary boat [is] in a museum alongside.

VALLEY OF THE KINGS

WEST VALLEY

Tomb of Amenhotep III

Tomb of Ay

LUXOR AND
THE WEST BANK
Sites on the Nile's west
bank include Medinet
Habu (the mortuary
temple of Ramses III),
Deir el-Medina (the village
of the workmen who built the royal
tombs), several monumental temples
(including the Ramesseum), and the
Valleys of the Kings and Queens.

EAST VALLEY

Tomb of
the Kings

Temple of Thutmose III

Temple of Hatshepsut

Temple of Mentuhotep

Temple of
Ramses IV

Temple
Thutmose

Temple of Ramses
(Ramesseum)

VALLEY OF THE QUEENS

Temple of Hathor

DEIR EL-MEDINA

Workman's
Village

Temple of Thutmose IV

Temple of Merenptah

Temple of Ay
and Horemheb

Temple of Ramses III

MEDINET
HABU

Memnon Colossi

N

◆ Temple of Thoth

0   0.5   1 mile

0   1 km

1 3 8

VALLEY OF THE KINGS

The many rock-cut tombs in this desolate valley include those of Tutankhamun (whose mummy has been returned to his burial chamber), Ramses VI (which has brightly painted walls), and Sety I (one of the deepest).

Temple of Sety I

COLOSSI OF MEMNON

A short ferry trip across the Nile from Luxor takes visitors to the West Bank. One of the first sights is nearly all that remains of Amenhotep III's mortuary temple – the massive Colossi of Memnon.

THE WEST BANK SITES

Karnak Temple

LUXOR

Luxor Temple

LUXOR

This modern city lies near the site of Thebes, the New Kingdom capital. In ancient times, the great temples of Karnak and Luxor were linked by an avenue of ram-headed sphinxes. Luxor Museum has a fine collection of antiquities.

KINGDOMS AND DYNASTIES

THE PHARAOHS ruled Egypt for more than 3,000 years. Historians usually divide this vast stretch of time into 31 dynasties. All the dates given in these tables are approximate.

DJOSER

EARLY DYNASTIC PERIOD 3100-2613 B.C.

FIRST DYNASTY
(3100-2690 B.C.)
Narmer
Aha
Djer
Djet
Den
Anedjib
Semerkhet
Qaa

SECOND DYNASTY
(2890-2686 B.C.)
Hotepsekhemwy
Nebra
Nynetjer
Peribsen
Khasekhem

OLD KINGDOM 2686-2160 B.C.

THIRD DYNASTY
(2686-2613 B.C.)
Sanakht
Djoser
Sekhemkhet
Khaba
Huni

FOURTH DYNASTY
(2613-2494 B.C.)
Sneferu
Khufu (Cheops)
Djedefra
Khafra (Chephren)
Menkaura (Mycerinus)
Shepseskaf

FIFTH DYNASTY
(2494-2345 B.C.)
Userkaf
Sahura
Neferirkara
Shepseskara
Neferefra
Nyuserra
Menkauhor
Djedkara
Unas

SIXTH DYNASTY
(2345-2181 B.C.)
Teti
Userkara
Pepy I
Merenra
Pepy II

SEVENTH/EIGHTH DYNASTIES
(2181-2125 B.C.)

FIRST INTERMEDIATE PERIOD 2160-2040 B.C.

NINTH DYNASTY
(2160-2130 B.C.)
TENTH DYNASTY
(2125-2025 B.C.)
Meryibra Khety
Wahkara Khety
Merykara

ELEVENTH DYNASTY (THEBES)
(2125-1985 B.C.)
Mentuhotep I
Intef I
Intef II
Intef III

MIDDLE KINGDOM 2040-1750 B.C.

ELEVENTH DYNASTY (Continued)
Mentuhotep II   2055-2004 B.C.

TWELFTH DYNASTY
(1985-1795 B.C.)
Amenemhat I   1985-1955 B.C.
Senusret I   1965-1920 B.C.
Amenemhat II   1922-1878 B.C.
Senusret II   1880-1874 B.C.
Senusret III   1874-1855 B.C.
Amenemhat III   1854-1808 B.C.
Amenemhat IV   1808-1799 B.C.
Sobekkara Sobekneferu
                 1799-1795 B.C.

SECOND INTERMEDIATE PERIOD 1750-1650 B.C.

THIRTEENTH DYNASTY
(1795-1650 B.C.)
Sobekhotep III
Sobekhotep IV
Neferhotep I

FOURTEENTH DYNASTY
(1750-1650 B.C.)

FIFTEENTH DYNASTY
(1650-1550 B.C.)
Khyan
Apepi

SIXTEENTH DYNASTY
(1650-1550 B.C.)

SEVENTEENTH DYNASTY
(1650-1550 B.C.)
Intef V
Taa I
Kamose

NEW KINGDOM
1550-1086 B.C.
EIGHTEENTH DYNASTY
(1550-1295 B.C.)

Ahmose I	1550-1525 B.C.
Amenhotep I	1525-1504 B.C.
Thutmose I	1504-1492 B.C.
Thutmose II	1492-1479 B.C.
Hatshepsut	1479-1457 B.C.
Thutmose III	1479-1425 B.C.
Amenhotep II	1427-1400 B.C.
Thutmose IV	1400-1390 B.C.
Amenhotep III	1390-1352 B.C.
Amenhotep IV	
(Akhenaten)	1352-1336 B.C.
Tutankhamun	1336-1327 B.C.
Ay	1327-1323 B.C.
Horemheb	1323-1295 B.C.

NINETEENTH DYNASTY
(1295-1186 B.C.)

Ramses I	1295-1294 B.C.
Sety I	1294-1279 B.C.
Ramses II	1279-1213 B.C.
Merenptah	1213-1203 B.C.
Sety II	1200-1194 B.C.
Saptah	1194-1188 B.C.
Tausret	1188-1186 B.C.

TWENTIETH DYNASTY
(1186-1069 B.C.)

Setnakht	1186-1184 B.C.
Ramses III	1184-1153 B.C.
Ramses IV	1153-1147 B.C.
Ramses V	1147-1143 B.C.
Ramses VI	1143-1136 B.C.
Ramses VII	1136-1129 B.C.
Ramses VIII	1129-1126 B.C.
Ramses IX	1126-1108 B.C.
Ramses X	1108-1099 B.C.
Ramses XI	1099-1069 B.C.

THIRD INTERMEDIATE
PERIOD
1086-661 B.C.
TWENTY-FIRST DYNASTY
(1069-945 B.C.)

Smendes	1069-1043 B.C.
Psusennes I	1039-991 B.C.
Amenemope	993-984 B.C.
Saamun	978-959 B.C.
Psusennes II	959-945 B.C.

TWENTY-SECOND DYNASTY
(945-715 B.C.)

Sheshonq I	945-924 B.C.
Osorkon I	924-889 B.C.
Takelot I	889-874 B.C.
Osorkon II	874-850 B.C.
Takelot II	850-825 B.C.
Sheshonq III	825-773 B.C.
Pimay	773-767 B.C.
Sheshonq V	767-730 B.C.

TWENTY-THIRD DYNASTY
(818-715 B.C.)

Padibast I	818-793 B.C.
Osorkon III	777-749 B.C.

TWENTY-FOURTH DYNASTY
(727-715 B.C.)

Tefnakht	

TWENTY-FIFTH DYNASTY
(NUBIAN KINGS)
(747-656 B.C.)

Piy	747-716 B.C.
Shabako	716-702 B.C.
Shabitko	702-690 B.C.
Taharqo	690-664 B.C.
Tanutamani	664-656 B.C.

LATE PERIOD
661-332 B.C.
TWENTY-SIXTH DYNASTY
(664-525 B.C.)

Psamtek I	664-610 B.C.
Nekau II	610-595 B.C.
Psamtek II	595-589 B.C.
Apries	589-570 B.C.
Amasis	570-526 B.C.
Psamtek III	526-525 B.C.

TWENTY-SEVENTH DYNASTY
(PERSIAN KINGS)
(525-404 B.C.)

Cambyses	525-522 B.C.
Darius I	522-486 B.C.
Xerxes	486-465 B.C.
Artaxerxes I	465-424 B.C.
Darius II	424-405 B.C.
Artaxerxes II	405-359 B.C.

TWENTY-EIGHTH DYNASTY
(404-399 B.C.)

Amyrtaeus	404-399 B.C.

TWENTY-NINTH DYNASTY
(399-380 B.C.)

Nepherites I	399-393 B.C.
Achoris	392-380 B.C.

THIRTIETH DYNASTY
(380-343 B.C.)

Nectanebo I	380-362 B.C.
Teos	362-360 B.C.
Nectanebo II	360-343 B.C.

THIRTY-FIRST DYNASTY
(PERSIAN KINGS)
(343-332 B.C.)

Artaxerxes III	343-338 B.C.
Arses	338-336 B.C.
Darius III	336-332 B.C.

GREEK PERIOD
332-30 B.C.

Alexander the Great	332-323 B.C.
Philip Arrhidaeus	323-317 B.C.
Alexander IV	317-305 B.C.
Ptolemy I	305-282 B.C.
Ptolemy II	284-246 B.C.
Ptolemy III	246-222 B.C.
Ptolemy IV	222-205 B.C.
Ptolemy V	205-180 B.C.
Ptolemy VI	180-145 B.C.
Ptolemy VII	145 B.C.
Ptolemy VIII	170-116 B.C.
Ptolemy IX	116-107 B.C.
Ptolemy X	107-88 B.C.
Ptolemy XI	80 B.C.
Ptolemy XII	80-51 B.C.
Cleopatra VII	51-30 B.C.

FAMOUS PHARAOHS

THE NAMES of more than one hundred pharaohs are known from inscriptions. But little is known about most of them. Much more is known about a few famous kings, like Ramses II, who covered temple walls with detailed accounts of his exploits. Royal mummies have also revealed many fascinating details.

DJOSER (C.2650 B.C.)
The earliest known reference to the sun god Ra is on a relief celebrating Djoser's name. This powerful king led expeditions to Sinai in search of turquoise. He built the first pyramid, the Step Pyramid at Saqqara. It has a network of underground chambers, where King Djoser was buried.

KHUFU (CHEOPS)
(2587-2564 B.C.)
Khufu built the Great Pyramid at Giza. This monumental feat must have been used nearly all of Egypt's workforce for about 20 years. Its treasures were robbed long ago. But in 1925, gilded furniture from the burial of Khufu's mother was discovered.

KHAFRA (CHEPHREN) (2556-2530 B.C.)
This pharaoh was the builder of the second pyramid at Giza, which is only 4 m (13 ft) shorter than Great Pyramid. Khafra succeeded Khufu and may well have been his younger brother. Khafra's pyramid is part of a complex of buildings, which includes a well-preserved valley temple, made from massive slabs of granite. The temple housed 23 life-size statues of the king. Amongst these was the famous seated statue of Khafra, the falcon god Horus perched on the back of his throne. Carved from diorite, it is now in Cairo Museum. The Great Sphinx, which crouches in front of the Giza complex, is thought to be a portrait of Khafra.

MENKAURA (MYCERINUS) (2526-2506 B.C.)
He built Giza's third pyramid (the smallest). The earliest known statue of a king and queen is Menkaura arm in arm with his favourite wife.

MENTUHOTEP II (2055-2004 B.C.)
He was a Theban prince and energetic warrior. In c.2040 B.C. he became founder of the Middle Kingdom when he conquered the north and re-united Egypt. He ruled for 51 years and was buried in a great rock tomb in the cliffs at Deir el-Bahri.

SENUSRET III (1874-1855 B.C.)
This Middle Kingdom pharaoh extended royal control over Egypt's many *nomes* (districts). He also conquered part of Nubia and developed the chain of massive mud-brick forts protecting Egypt's southern border.

HATSHEPSUT (1479-1457 B.C.)
Hatshepsut was the first woman pharaoh. She married her half-brother, Thutmose II, and ruled alongside him, holding most of the power.
When he died, her step-son Thutmose III took the throne. But he was still a child, so Hatshepsut ruled Egypt until her death. She pursued peaceful policies, building up the economy instead of fighting her neighbours. She opened new turquoise mines, sent a trading expedition to Punt, and erected two obelisks at Karnak. On the walls of her temple at Deir el-Bahri, she had herself portrayed as a man, with a false beard and all the other symbols of kingship.

THUTMOSE III (1479-1425 B.C.)
After his step-mother's death, Thutmose III became a powerful warrior king, extending Egyptian power deep into Asia. He added to the great temple to Amun at Karnak and erected obelisks, including *Cleopatra's Needle* – now in London.

AMENHOTEP III
(1390-1352 B.C.)

This pharaoh ruled a huge empire at the height of its wealth. He built the Colossi of Memnon and Luxor temple. He also added to Karnak temple. His new palace at Malkata was next to the world's first known chariot racetrack.

AKHENATEN (1352-1336 B.C.)

Crowned Amenhotep IV, the "heretic pharaoh" took a great interest in the sun god Aten. After six years as king, he changed his name to Akhenaten in the god's honour. His new religion was the first in history to worship a single god. He created a new city, Akhetaten, at Amarna. Here, art flourished in new, original styles, and lavish offerings were made to Aten. The pharaoh closed the traditional temples, depriving many priests of their power. He also ignored affairs of state, and the normally efficient Egyptian government was in chaos. When he died, his city was abandoned and his statues defaced. His wife Nefertiti may have ruled on alone.

TUTANKHAMUN
(1336-1327 B.C.)

The old gods were restored under Akhenaten's successor, the boy-king Tutankhamun. His father was probably Akhenaten. Another wife, Kiya, is more likely to have been his mother than Nefertiti. For most of the pharaoh's nine-year reign, power lay with an army general (Horemheb) and an elderly official (Ay). Both went on to rule Egypt after Tutankhamun died at age 18 or 19. His mummy shows skull damage, and some experts think he may have been murdered by Ay. He would barely have been remembered at all had his intact tomb full of glittering treasures not been found in 1922.

HOREMHEB (1323-1295 B.C.)

This king was a successful army general, who took the throne after the death

of Tutankhamun's elderly successor Ay. He banned the Aten religion and set about erasing the names of "heretics" Akhenaten and Tutankhamun (born Tutankhaten).

SETY I
(1294-1279 B.C.)
Great war leader Sety I revived Egypt's expansion policy in the East by marching into Syria and driving back the Hittites. In 1817, his splendid Theban tomb was discovered. His well-preserved mummy is in Cairo Museum.

TAHARQO
(690-664 B.C.)
The most famous Nubian king of Egypt, Taharqo is mentioned in the Bible. He revived classic traditions in art and followed Egyptian gods. Ousted by Assyrian invaders, he was buried in a pyramid in Nubia (Sudan).

RAMSES II (1279-1213 B.C.)
Known as Ramses the Great, this king fought an indecisive battle with the Hittites, then signed the world's first official peace treaty. In the 60 peaceful years that followed, he built many monuments to celebrate his "victory". Ramses II had more than 100 children. His mummy shows that he was very tall.

CLEOPATRA VII (51-30 B.C.)
The last Ptolemaic pharaoh and the only one to speak Egyptian, Cleopatra tried to prevent Rome taking over Egypt. She had an affair with the Roman general Julius Caesar, and they had a son. After Caesar's death, she fell in love with another Roman general, Mark Antony. They had three children and planned to rule a mighty kingdom together. But they were defeated by Octavian, Antony's political rival. Octavian pursued them to Egypt, where Antony killed himself after receiving a false report of Cleopatra's death. She surrendered to Octavian. But when she could not win him over, she committed suicide – legend says, by clasping a poisonous asp (cobra) to her breast.

RAMSES III
(1184-1153 B.C.)
He saved Egypt from a series of foreign invasions and fought against corruption. Court

members, including one of his wives, tried to poison him. They were tried and forced to kill themselves. A second plot may have succeeded; he died a year later.

GODS OF ANCIENT EGYPT

DIFFERENT GODS AND GODDESSES were popular at different times, and most changed their character over the centuries. Here are a few of ancient Egypt's most important deities.

KHNUM
Creator god Khnum was worshipped as a ram or a ram-headed man. He was said to mould children on a potter's wheel, then plant them in their mother's body.

GEB
One myth tells that the earth god Geb and his wife, sky goddess Nut, created the sun, which is reborn each day. Geb is shown with a goose, the hieroglyph for his name.

PTAH
The centre of worship for this god was Memphis. The city priests maintained that Ptah was the supreme god, who created all the other gods by speaking their names.

ANUBIS
Jackal-headed Anubis was god of the dead and mummification. He watched over the mummy and supervised many funerary rites.

NEPHTHYS
This goddess was the sister of Isis, and she helped Isis resurrect the mutilated body of Osiris. The two sisters are usually shown together. They protected coffins and canopic jars, often in the form of a pair of hawks.

SOBEK
This crocodile god was ruler of the water, and the Nile was said to be his sweat. The main centres of worship were places where the danger of crocodile attacks was high.

ABYDOS TRIAD

Triads were small families of gods worshipped in a particular area. The family consisted of a husband, wife, and son. The Abydos triad was Osiris, his wife Isis, and their son, the sky god Horus.

HORUS ISIS OSIRIS

KHONS MUT AMUN

THEBAN TRIAD

The chief god worshipped at the temples of Karnak and Luxor was the creator god Amun. His wife Mut was a war goddess, sometimes shown as a vulture or a lioness. Their son was Khons, a moon god, often depicted as a mummy.

FORMS OF MAAT

Many gods took various forms in different times or settings. Here are three representations of the goddess Maat, who stood for justice, truth, and order. In each of these forms, she is wearing the *Feather of Truth* on her head.

HATHOR

This goddess of the sky and of love was associated with the cow. She was often shown with horns that held the sun.

THOTH

A patron of scribes and the god of wisdom and writing, Thoth was also a moon god. He was depicted as an ibis or a baboon.

HIEROGLYPHS

EGYPTIAN picture-writing
is called hieroglyphs, which
means "sacred symbols" in
Greek. The symbols could
have various meanings.

*Symbol is
used for
these sounds*

The alphabet

Every word was written exactly as it
was pronounced, although only in
consonants. Vowels were omitted. The
alphabet consisted of 24 hieroglyphs,
each representing a single sound.

*Owl faces right,
so read right to left*

*This is a weak
consonant,
not a vowel*

READING THE RIGHT WAY
A hieroglyphic text could be read from left
to right, right to left, or top to bottom. The
symbols of animals or people tell you which
way to read – always read towards the faces.

W MOON UNDER WICK — QUAIL CHICK	**TH** THree — COW'S BELLY	**Y,I** YOUNG INK KITE — REED LEAF
J JUNK GIN — SNAKE	**T** — LOAF OF BREAD	**B** — LEG
G GAP — POT STAND	**P** — MAT	**TH** THAT — UNKNOWN
N — WATER	**D** — HAND	**M** — OWL
F,V — HORNED VIPER	**K** — HILL	**H** — TWISTED FLAX
H — REED HUT	**L,R** — MOUTH	**M**AY **A** — ARM
A,E,O — VULTURE	**Z** — DOOR BOLT	CHIP **CH** — TETHERING ROPE
S — FOLDED CLOTH	**SH** — POND	**K** — BASKET

GROUP SIGNS

To save time, many hieroglyphs represent not one, but two or even three sounds together. For example, instead of spelling "sa" with two hieroglyphs, one for each of the separate sounds, it could be spelt with one symbol, a duck.

DUCK
= S+A = SA

BEETLE
= KH+P+R= KHEPER

HOUSE
= P+R = PER

TABLE WITH BREAD
= H+T+P = HOTEP

ARRANGING SYMBOLS

Symbols that made up a word did not have to be in a line; they could be fitted together in several ways, to please the eye.

TWO WAYS
TO WRITE
"QUEEN"

DETERMINATIVES

Some symbols are like clues. These are determinatives. They were added to the text to make the meaning clear, but they were not read as sounds.

PERSON   WALK, RUN   SEE   PLURAL

CLUE

Here is an example of a determinative. A scribe's pallete had two meanings. Next to a figure of a man it read "scribe", but next to a roll of papyrus it meant "to write".

FIGHTING EVIL

Egyptians thought symbols had power for good or evil. Scribes sometimes cut the heads off snakes or drew hawks with no claws to protect themselves from any harm.

GOOD LUCK
Symbols like the *Wadjet* Eye were thrown in for good luck.

EGYPTIAN NUMERALS

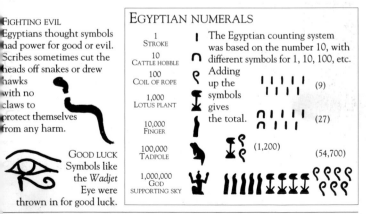

1 STROKE		
10 CATTLE HOBBLE		
100 COIL OF ROPE		
1,000 LOTUS PLANT		
10,000 FINGER		
100,000 TADPOLE		
1,000,000 GOD SUPPORTING SKY		

The Egyptian counting system was based on the number 10, with different symbols for 1, 10, 100, etc. Adding up the symbols gives the total.

(9)

(27)

(1,200)

(54,700)

ARCHITECTURE

THE SURVIVING buildings of ancient Egypt are mostly religious, either temples or tombs. Their forms symbolize natural cycles and beliefs.

COLONNADE
Long colonnades were a feature of many temples. This one with palm-tree capitals is from Philae.

ARTISTIC LICENCE
Some of the highly elaborate architectural forms depicted in tomb paintings were obviously exaggerated.

PLANT FORMS
These Old Kingdom columns are shaped like papyrus stems (left) and a palm tree (right).

CARVED
Square pillars were sculpted with figures of gods and men, some massive, in relief or even in the round. This is the god Osiris.

Opening bud

Decorated with images of gods

CAPITAL FROM THE TEMPLE OF ESNA

COLUMN
Temple columns could be fluted or smooth. But most were sculpted, often with elaborate reliefs that were then painted.

HIGH GATEWAY (MEDINET HABU)

Ramses III's mortuary temple and palace are enclosed within massive, 10 m (33 ft) thick walls. This ruined gateway was the main entrance to this Theban complex.

Window

KING'S HAREM

Some of rooms in the three-storey gateway were used as a harem. Walls show scenes of Ramses III being attended by young women.

Detail from the painted pavement at Akhenaten's palace

FLOOR FRESCOES

The walls and floors of palaces and villas were plastered and painted with bright frescoes of patterns or nature scenes. These are from Akhenaten's palace.

AKHENATEN'S PALACE AT AMARNA

Nothing but ruined foundations of this palace remain. But it can be imagined from paintings in the tomb of high priest Meryre. This reconstructed storage area was just a small part of the vast palace complex, which was set amongst landscaped gardens with many trees and shady pools.

MUSEUMS

THE FOLLOWING is only a partial list of museums where ancient Egyptian artefacts can be seen. Many more exist throughout the world.

UNITED KINGDOM
Ashmolean Museum
Beaumont Street
Oxford OX1 2PH

Birmingham Museum
Chamberlain Square
Birmingham B3 3DH

Bolton Museum
Le Mans Crescent
Bolton
Lancashire BL1 1SA

British Museum
Great Russell Street
London WC1B 3DG
The biggest and most comprehensive collection outside Egypt, including the Rosetta Stone and more than 80 mummies

Durham University Oriental Museum
Elvet Hill
Durham DH1 3TH

Fitzwilliam Museum
Trumpington Street
Cambridge CB2 1RB

Glasgow Museum
Kelvingrove
Glasgow G3 8AG

Liverpool Museum
William Brown Street
Liverpool L3 8EN

Manchester Museum
The University of Manchester
Oxford Road
Manchester M13 9PL

National Museum of Scotland
Chambers Street
Edinburgh EH1 1JF

Petrie Museum of Egyptian Archaeology
University College
London
Gower Street
London WC1E 6BT

Wellcome Museum
University College
Singleton Park
Swansea SA2 8PP

AUSTRALIA
Australian Museum
Sydney

National Gallery of Victoria
Melbourne

Nicholson Museum of Antiquities
Sydney

South Australian Museum
Adelaide

AUSTRIA
Kunsthistorisches Museum
Vienna

BELGIUM
Musées Royaux d'Art et d'Histoire
Brussels

CANADA
McGill University Ethnology Museum
Montreal

Royal Ontario Museum
Toronto

CZECH REPUBLIC
Náprstkovo Museum
Prague

DENMARK
Nationalmuseet
Copenhagen

EGYPT
Egyptian Museum
Cairo
*By far the best collection in
the world, including the
treasures of Tutankhamun*

Greco-Roman Museum
Alexandria

Luxor Museum
Luxor

FRANCE
Louvre
Paris
*Outside Egypt, only the
British Museum has a
bigger collection*

GERMANY
Ägyptisches Museum
Berlin
*Houses many artefacts from
Akhenaten's city Amarna,
incuding the famous bust
of Nefertiti*

Ägyptisches Museum
Leipzig

**Roemer-Pelizaeus
Museum**
Hildesheim

GREECE
**National Archaeological
Museum**
Athens

IRELAND
**National Museum
of Ireland**
Dublin

ITALY
Museo Archeologico
Florence

Museo Egizio
Turin
*One of the best collections
in Europe*

Museo Egizio
Vatican City, Rome

JAPAN
**University
Archaeological Museum**
Kyoto

THE NETHERLANDS
**Rijksmuseum van
Oudheden**
Leiden

POLAND
Museum Narodowe
Warsaw

RUSSIA
Pushkin Museum
Moscow

The Hermitage Museum
St. Petersburg

SUDAN
National Museum
Khartum
*Antiquities from both
ancient Nubia and Egypt*

SWEDEN
Medelhavsmuseet
Stockholm

UNITED STATES
**Boston Museum of
Fine Arts**
Boston, Mass.

Brooklyn Museum
Brooklyn, New York

**Metropolitan Museum
of Art**
New York
*The best collection in
the Americas*

**The University of
Pennsylvanie Museum**
Philadelphia, Pa.

Glossary

AMULET
A lucky charm, worn or carried to ward off evil.

ANKH
A kind of amulet, it was the symbol of life. Only gods and kings are shown holding the ankh.

BA
A person's spirit or soul, thought to live on after death. The *Ba* is often depicted as a human-headed bird.

BOOK OF THE DEAD
A collection of up to 200 spells, placed with the mummy to help the deceased reach the other world safely.

CANOPIC JARS
Four jars used to hold the embalmed stomach, liver, lungs, and intestines.

CARNELIAN
A red semi-precious gemstone.

CARTOUCHE
A hieroglyphic symbol representing an oval-shaped loop. A pharaoh's name was written inside the cartouche.

CATARACT
A stretch of rapids that interrupt the Nile's flow.

CAUSEWAY
A raised road or path.

COLOSSUS
A larger than life-size statue, usually of a king. They are often found outside temples.

DELTA
The flat area at the mouth of a river, where the mainstream splits into marshy branches.

DEMOTIC
Developed from hieratic writing, this cursive form is found on Egyptian monuments and papyri.

DYNASTY
A succession of rulers from related families. Egypt's pharaohs formed 31 dynasties.

FAIENCE
A glazed earthenware.

FALSE DOOR
A symbolic gateway carved or painted on tombs and coffins, through which a dead person's spirit was thought to pass.

HIERATIC
A form of writing adapted from hieroglyphs. It was written on papyrus using an ink and brush.

KOHL
Black eye make-up worn by Egyptian men, women, and children.

LOWER EGYPT
The northern part of Egypt around the Nile Delta.

MUMMY
When an Egyptian died, the body was turned into a mummy. To do this, it was dried, preserved, and wrapped in linen.

MUMMY CASE
A coffin containing the mummified remains of an ancient Egyptian.

NATRON
A salt that occurs naturally in Egypt. It was used to purify and dry out the body when it was being mummified.

NECROPOLIS
A Greek word that means "city of the dead". It is used to describe Egyptian cemeteries.

NOME
A province of ancient Egypt – it was divided into areas to make government easier.

OBELISK
A tapering four-sided pillar made of stone.

OSTRACON
A flake of limestone or broken pottery that was used for writing or making rough sketches on.

PAPYRUS
A water reed used to make a kind of paper. It was the main writing material used in Egypt.

PECTORAL
A piece of jewellery that was worn on the chest.

PHARAOH
An Egyptian king. The word means "The Great House", the royal palace.

PUNT
A semi-mythical land that Egyptian texts refer to as a source for trade. Its exact location is still unclear, but it was south of Egypt, perhaps in Somalia.

PYLON
The monumental entrance wall of a temple.

PYRAMID
A huge tomb with a square base and four sloping sides, built to house a pharaoh when he died.

PYRAMID TEXTS
Religious writings carved on the walls inside a pyramid. They are an early version of the *Book of the Dead*, a collection of spells to help the dead pharaoh reach the next world.

RELIEF
A carved or moulded sculpture that stands out from its background.

SARCOPHAGUS
A stone coffin that is either rectangular or human-shaped. The word means "flesh-eater" in Greek.

SCARAB
An Egyptian dung-beetle, symbol of rebirth.

SHABTI
From an Egyptian word meaning "to answer", this mummy-shaped figurine was placed in the tomb with a mummy. When the dead were called upon to work in the next life, they would call

their *shabtis*, who they believed would answer and do the work instead.

SPHINX
A statue in the shape of a lion with the head of a man or ram. A sphinx was a symbol of royal power.

STELA
A slab of stone (or sometimes wood) with text and pictures, set up in a tomb or temple.

UPPER EGYPT
The southern part of ancient Egypt. The main city was Thebes.

URAEUS
The royal cobra, worn by the pharaoh on his brow. It was thought to spit fire at the pharaoh's enemies.

VALLEY OF THE KINGS
A desolate valley on the west bank of the Nile near Luxor, which contains the tombs of many of the New Kingdom pharaohs.

VIZIER
The chief minister. He looked after government departments responsible for running the country and reported to the pharaoh every day.

Index

Acknowledgements

Dorling Kindersley would like to thank:
Hilary Bird for the index; Sarah Ponder for design assistance; Suzanne Melia for editorial assistance; Caroline Brooke for editorial research; Caroline Potts for picture research assistance; James Anderson and Yak El-Droubie for cartography; The British Museum for supplying references for the Dynasties, pages 140/141 and to The Metropolitan Museum New York for supplying references for the hieroglyphs, pages 148/149.

Photographs by:
Peter Anderson, Geoff Brightling, Christi Graham, Peter Hayman, Alan Hills, Dave King, Nick Nicholls, Kim Sayer, Ivor Kerslake, Karl Shone.

Illustrations by:
Peter Anderson, Russell Barnett, Stephen Conlin, Peter Dennis, Dave Donkin, Simone End, Eugene Fleury, Will Giles, Thomas Keenes, Sandra Pond, Sarah Ponder, Peter Visscher, J. G. Wilkinson, John Woodcock.

Picture Credits
t top; *c* centre; *a* above; *b* below; *l* left; *r* right.

The Publisher would like to thank the following for their kind permission to reproduce their photographs:

Ashmolean Museum, Oxford 45cra,cr,crb, 60tr;/The Griffith Institute 125tl,ca,cr; Bolton Museum (jacket), 2br, 3tr, 14br, 25tr, 29tl, 30b, 88/9, 101br, 107tr, 113cr, 119c; Bridgeman Art Library 63br, 74/5br;/Louvre, Paris 56bl;/The British Museum 68cr; The British Library/ Laurence Pordes 16cr; The British Museum 1c, 2tl, tr,bl, 3l,br, 5t, 7br, 13r, 14bl, 15cb,

16b, 17tl,cl, 18tr,c,bl, 19b, 22tr, 22/23b, 23br, 29tc, 31tl,tr,cr, 32tr,b, 33tl,c,br, 34cl,clb, 36bl, 37br,tc, 39bc,tl, 40/41tc, 46/47b, 46tl,cr, 47tr,c,tl, 48/49bl, 49tl,(jacket), 51bc, 52br, 56cr, 57c, 58bl, 59r,c,cl, 60cb, bl,tl, 61tl,r,bl,bc, 62br, 63tl, 64/5c, 70tl, c,br, 71tr,cla,br, 73t, 76tl,bl, 77tl,c,br, 80cr, 81br,bl, 82c, 83t,ca,(jacket), 84c,cl,cr,(jacket), 85tr,bl,crb,cr, 93tr, 94tl, 95br, 96tr, 97cl,c, 98/99, 100bl,r, 101tl, 103l,tr,(jacket), 104tl, 105tr, 106tr, 107bc, (jacket),br,tc,cl, 109tr, 110/11tc, 110bl,br, 111bl, 112l, 114tl,cl,br,bl, 115tl,cr,bc,br,tr, 116tr,b, 117cr, 118tr,bl,cl, 119b,tl, 120cl, 121tl,ca,tr,bl, 128/9b, 129tl,tr, 131tl, 132l,cr,bc; Cairo Museum 20bl,br; Lester Cheeseman 24cr, 131r; Peter Clayton 57br, 125bc; Robert Harding Picture Library 102bl; Michael Holford 102cl, 105c; The Manchester Museum 19tl,tc,tr, 24bl, 31b, 37cr,tl,(jacket), 55tr, 56bc, 57tl,tr, 68/69bc, 69cr, 80tl,cl,bl, 81ca,(jacket), 84tl, 92tr,(jacket),cl,cr, 93tl, cr,br, 101cl,(jacket), 102tr, 105tc, 106bl,bc, 108tr,cra,bl, 108/109bc, 109br, 111br, 112cr, 113tl, 117tl,tr,br, 118br, 120br,l, 131c, 133tl, tr; Metropolitan Museum New York 90/91bc, John G. Ross 10/11, 14tr, 15tl, 16tl, 20c, 21tc,br, 22cl, 23tl, 25b, 28tl, 29r, 35tr,br, 37bc, 38br, 39cl, 40br, 41cla,br, 45b, 66/7, 74/85tl, 90c,tr, 94br, 95c, 96bl, cr, 97br,tr, 104br, 111tr, 112/3b, 122cr, 123tl,tr,cr, 122/3b, 124l,cr,b, 125tr, 126/7, 130bl;/Rapho 34cr, 38clb; The Science Museum 53br; Lin White 12tr,cr, 13tl, 25tl, 38tl, 39r, 41bc, 78/79, 90bl, 105br, 109tl, 113tr, 122cl, 128c, 130cr, 131bl, 133bl, 139tr,cr.

Every effort has been made to trace the copyright holders and we apologise in advance for any unintentional omissions. We would be pleased to insert the appropriate acknowledgement in any subsequent edition of this publication.